PET JOBS 101

HOW TO CHOOSE YOUR DREAM JOB AND JUMPSTART YOUR BUSINESS

WENDY VAN DE POLL

SPIRIT PAW PRESS, LLC

Pet Jobs 101:
How to Choose your Dream Job and
Jumpstart Your Business

Copyright © 2019 by Wendy Van de Poll

All rights reserved. All rights reserved. No part of this publication may be reproduced, distributed, or transmitted in any form or by any means, including photocopying, recording, or other electronic or mechanical methods, without the prior written permission of the publisher, except in the case of brief quotations embodied in reviews and certain other non-commercial uses permitted by copyright law.

Published by Spirit Paw Press, LLC, Concord, NH, 03303

Publisher's Cataloging-in-Publication Data
provided by Five Rainbows Cataloging Services

Names: Van de Poll, Wendy, author.
Title: Pet jobs 101 : the pet biz series / Wendy Van de Poll.
Description: Concord, NH : Spirit Paw Press, 2019. | Series: Pet biz, bk. 2. | Also available in ebook format.
Identifiers: ISBN 978-1-7324375-4-8 (paperback)
Subjects: LCSH: Pets. | Pet industry. | Pets--Services for. | Home-based businesses. | Authorship--Vocational guidance. | BISAC: PETS / General. | BUSINESS & ECONOMICS / Home-Based Businesses.
Classification: LCC SF414.7 .V36 2019 (print) | LCC SF414.7 (ebook) | DDC 636.0887/0681--dc23.

THANK YOU

THANK YOU

A Free Gift

Thank you for purchasing *Pet Jobs 101: How to Choose Your Dream Job and Jumpstart Your Business.* To show my appreciation, I am offering a free gift to help you with choosing your new career.

A Free Downloadable List of
Over 150 links to Pet Careers, Organizations and much more!

Your link to receive your Free Gift!

https://wendyvandepoll.com/pet-jobs-free-gift

THANK YOU

THANK YOU

A Free Gift

Thank you for purchasing *Pet Jobs 101: How to Choose Your Dream Job and Jumpstart Your Business*. To show my appreciation, I am offering a free gift to help you with choosing your new career.

A Free Downloadable List of
Over 150 links to Pet Careers, Organizations and much more!

Your link to receive your Free Gift!

https://wendyvandepoll.com/pet-jobs-free-gift

*To all those who believe animals make
the world spectacular.*

CONTENTS

Introduction   ix

SECTION I
ONLINE PET JOBS

1. Pet Blogger and Pet Book Writer   3
2. Drop Shipping and Online Stores   8
3. Animal Communicator   16
4. Pet Loss Grief Mentor   21
5. Online Course Creator   27
6. Pet Portrait Artist   33
7. Pet T-Shirt Designer   37
8. Pet Brand Creator   41

SECTION II
IN PERSON PET JOBS

9. Pet Photographer   49
10. Professional Pet Sitter   53
11. Dog Trainer   58
12. Groomer   62
13. Pet Bakery   67
14. Animal Energy Practitioner   72
15. Kennel Owner   77
16. Pet Massage Therapist   82
17. Doggie Day Care Owner   86
18. Veterinarian   90
19. Veterinary Technician   94
20. Barn Manager   98
21. Veterinary Acupuncturist   102
22. Veterinarian Chiropractor   106

SECTION III
VOLUNTEER

23. Humane Society/Rescue Volunteer	113
24. Service Animal Trainer	118
25. Prison Dog Trainer/Handler	123
26. Foster Parent	127
27. Wildlife Rehabilitator	132

SECTION IV
JUMPSTART YOUR PET BUSINESS

28. Deciding What You Want to Do	139
29. Getting Started	146
30. Creating Your Website	161
31. Developing Your Website	165

SECTION V
CUSTOMER SERVICE TIPS

32. Handling Aggressive and Difficult Animals	175
33. Handling Difficult People	180
34. Building Customer Loyalty	187

Pep Talk!	195
Glossary	197
Resources	201
Epilogue	207
About the Author	209
Thank You!	211
Also by Wendy Van de Poll	213

INTRODUCTION

Are you unhappy with your current career? Would you like to work in the pet industry but don't know where to begin? Would you love to land your dream job in the pet industry but have no idea what that is yet?

The answers to your questions are not that far away. The truth is your passion and love for animals can easily grow into a full-time job. With the help from *Pet Jobs 101: How to Choose Your Dream Job and Jumpstart Your Business*, you will get the support and guidance you need to get started.

I am living proof that you can do it. Working within the pet industry is incredibly fun and rewarding. You get to work with your favorite animals and help their people make better choices. You carve out your own place within a special community of pet lovers—united across the world by their shared devotion to the furry (or feathered or scaled) companions. When I go to bed happy at the end of a long workday, I can easily say it is the best feeling in the world. And I can't wait to share this feeling with you.

From the time I was a little girl, I knew I wanted to work with animals. I loved animals—especially dogs, cats, horses, and goats. I just couldn't imagine a different career path. As a licensed massage therapist for humans, horses, and hounds, I have over thirty years' experience working in the holistic animal field. I am the successful owner of CenterForPetLoss-Grief.com, a pet blogger, author of over twelve best-selling pet books, and an entrepreneur of a business centered around

Introduction

holistic healing for pets and their people. I can honestly say I have made my dreams come true.

Furthermore, the pet industry is quite lucrative and continues to grow with opportunities. It is more than possible to make a living, and, in fact, your business can flourish. Exponential projected growth in this industry will ensure that your business endures and continues to be successful for years to come.

The knowledge I am doing my part to make the world a better place for animals means so much to me. I would love for you to experience that, too. There is nothing better than to hear former clients thanking me for what I did for their beloved companions.

Because I am so confident you can make your dreams come true, I urge you to first believe in yourself. You can do it! The second part is finding out which dream job is yours, and the third is jump-starting your business.

How to Get the Most From This Book:

1. Read the entire book cover to cover. Make some brief notes of the points I raise to be successful.
2. Pick out the career or careers you are interested in. Do some research and pick one career that meets the criteria for your dream job.
3. Do the action steps for each chapter. They are designed to help you become laser focused when choosing your dream job and jump-starting your pet business.

With this book, I will show you the ins and outs of many different pet businesses and countless options to enter the pet industry. I intend to help you through the stages of opening a pet business. I will also share how to find your dream job in the pet industry and thrive.

When you read this book, you will learn various ways in which you can live your dream. Don't wait to move forward with your inspiration—especially if you love pets and want to make a difference in the world. Working in the pet industry is extremely rewarding.

Read on and make the business of your dreams come true.

It is time to make a change and…

- Be happy with your new career.
- Know exactly what goes into a pet business.
- Land your dream job with confidence!

Affiliate links are present at the end of this book. This means if you purchase the product, I receive a small commission (which helps me greatly as an author.) You are not charged more because of the affiliate link. In fact, sometimes there is even a small discount. I have personally tested all affiliate products mentioned. I would never recommend something I didn't love.

SECTION I

ONLINE PET JOBS

Do you want to work from home? Are you ready to set your own hours?

Today, most businesses are online or have an online presence. With more and more people turning to the Internet every day, you must carve out your place on the web.

If you want to start an online business (and work in your pajamas!), you have access to a vast market of millions all around the world. But you must make yourself stand out because the competition can be stiff!

Read on to learn about the first group of careers—online pet businesses.

1

PET BLOGGER AND PET BOOK WRITER

Do you love writing? If so, a career in pet writing may be for you! People want information about how to care for their pets, and they want pet stories to warm their hearts. You can find a place for yourself in this industry by selling information, products, and stories through a blog or pet books.

Pet Blogging

In my book *Pet Blogging 101: How to Start a Riveting Pet Blog and Gain Loyal Followers*, I shared ways to start your own money-making pet blog. Blogging is certainly a viable career in the pet industry. You can generate income through a blog in many ways, from selling products to offering courses to hosting ads (Glossary) and affiliate links (Glossary) to other businesses you trust.

To start a blog, you must have a website. Set up your blog to fit a specific niche. Find a topic that interests you. It could be an informational blog, a blog about your adorable pooch, or a blog about animal rights that circulates important petitions pertaining to your cause.

Post content regularly. The more you post, the more active people will stay on your blog and the more relevant you stay in the online community. Be sure to stay on topic—you don't want to write about dogs on a tropical fish blog. Your readers come to expect something specific from you, so always deliver it.

When you start your blog, you want to become active on social media. That way you can find followers and update them about new content on your blog. You also want to collect email addresses on your blog so that you can send regular updates.

You don't need to have a degree in English to be a pet blogger. All you have to do is double-check your writing for grammatical and spelling errors with a software like ProWritingAid. As long as you write from the heart, you will find an audience who appreciates your content.

You can look at other blogs to see what sells—or what no one else is doing. Then you can either contribute to a popular niche or create a niche of your own that stands out from the competition with its originality.

Pet Book Writing

You can also write a book. Writing about animals can be a lucrative way to share your insights and knowledge with many readers. This is one of my favorite jobs, and in my book *Pet Authorpreneur 101: How to Become a Successful Pet Author and Grow Your Business,* I share the ins and outs of how to write a book.

From warm, fuzzy puppy stories to poetry to informational texts—books can definitely help you establish a brand (if that is your goal) and an income.

There are a couple of ways to approach authorship. You can write in a specific genre or niche that will benefit your existing business or start a new business around your book. The other option is to create a career where you are primarily an author. All options are profitable—just make sure you are clear with your business goals.

People will buy books that have great branding (Glossary), look professional, and offer helpful solutions. Find something you want to write about, and then write about it.

For example, you can create a non-fiction book that is based on your expertise and includes case studies or a fiction book that engages and entertains. You can even compile your blog into a well-rounded book. The possibilities are endless.

If you worry about your writing skills, please keep in mind you don't need to be a stellar writer! That is what editors and proofreaders are for. If you don't have the time or skills to put your thoughts on paper, you can hire a ghostwriter.

Honestly, you just need a story to tell.

Self-publishing is a lucrative way to reach an audience easily. With Amazon, you can format and publish your book in both paperback and Kindle formats. Smashwords (Resources) is another viable option. You can try the traditional route of publishing, but self-publishing guarantees that your wonderful book won't be rejected!

You will have to market your book on social media and through your blog or website to let people know about it. Plus, you will also need to urge people to leave reviews on Amazon so other readers feel more inclined to read your book—and so it rates well on Amazon algorithms (Glossary).

Important Considerations

Writing is something you can do from the comfort of your home. But it is not always as easy as it sounds. You must stay on top of marketing and research, know how to use keywords in your blog, and post to social media often.

You can make a full-time career from a blog. Just be prepared to work your full-time job until you have the funds to quit.

Writing a book for pet peeps is fun and can be lucrative. At the time of writing this book, I have over twelve best-selling books, and my royalties are significant.

Expected Salary: $19,000–$79,000 a year

Wrap-Up

Pet blogs and books are excellent mediums for artistic expression. Don't let fear of failure stop you from writing from your heart and reaching at least one person who loves what you have to say.

Writing about animals is a great way to reach an audience, make a difference in the pet industry, and express yourself.

While it takes some work, it is a financially lucrative career. If you write a pet book, you can self-publish it, market it with little money, and become an authority on pet-related topics.

If writing isn't your passion, or if you only want to make blogging a side gig, then read Chapter 2 to learn about starting a wildly successful pet product business! But first, visit your first set of action steps to determine if writing is the career for you.

Your First Action Steps

1. Do a search of animal blogs and books on a topic that interests you. Make a list of what excites you about their blog. What do you like about the content, topic, design, and colors?
2. If there isn't anything you like about the animal blogs and books you found, keep going with your research.
3. Consider online training for blog creation.
4. Check out options for self-publishing. I listed an awesome one in the Resources section of this book.
5. If you have always wanted to write but are experiencing self-doubt, make a list of what is holding you back, then tuck your list away and move ahead. Remember what I told you in the introduction? You can do it!

2

DROP SHIPPING AND ONLINE STORES

Do you like to shop? You may have already noticed the plethora of pet products offered by many different sellers on Amazon. Online shopping platforms are a shopper's paradise, and pet products are a huge business.

Online pet stores offer shoppers the convenience of comparing reviews and ordering items from the comfort of their homes. If you want to get in on this lucrative business, you can absolutely start an online pet product business.

Pet products account for a billion-dollar industry, and you can join in by having an online pet product retail shop. There are a few ways to go about this, but none of them entail owning a large warehouse, spending tons of money, or even leaving the comfort of your home!

Drop Shipping

Drop shipping does not mean you produce the products yourself. Instead, you obtain products from other companies and sell them. You make a profit and don't have many associated costs. Basically, you skip the middleman and don't have any products in stock.

Say you want to sell a high-quality pet food. You don't need to order ten thousand bags of food and store it in your home. Instead, you advertise the food on your website, and when a customer orders it, you refer the order to a wholesaler or manufacturer. The wholesaler will then ship it to your customer. You can markup items from the wholesale price in order to make a profit.

The first step is to create your business concept (Chapter 28). You're not just selling anything and everything pet-related. You find something you are passionate about—for example, caring for reptiles. Then, you build a brand around reptiles and your experiences with them. You should have a mission, like "removing stigmas around snakes" or "avoiding common mistakes new reptile owners make."

It is usually best to shape your brand around a certain marketable group. In the above example, your group might be people who are new to owning snakes. You want to direct your marketing to this group with hooks like: "If you are new to owning snakes, we have you covered!" You want to post ads that will appeal to this group, as well. If your demographic includes young people, for instance, you might post ads with lots of Internet slang and funny gifs. For an older demographic, you might avoid these things.

Next, figure out what products your demographic would want to buy. Look at Amazon and its trending categories. Then look at top products in the categories. This gives you an idea of what is selling now. You will want to focus on offering those products. You also want to visit Google Keyword Planner (Glossary) to see items people search for the most and tailor your drop shipping business around that information.

Next, you research suppliers of products you trust. For smaller businesses, you can visit their website and contact them directly about creating a drop shipping arrangement.

Drop shipping directly can be challenging for people new to selling this way, but there are marketplaces that make drop shipping easier. Visit a marketplace like AliExpress, Spocket, Printful, Doba, and Oberlo, or find your preferred retailers (Resources).

Within these marketplaces, you can create a shop and find products you want to sell. As you market these products, you pay the wholesale cost for each order and make a profit on however much you mark up the item. The items never come to you, so you don't ever have to stock them.

You can create your own website. Or you can use an inexpensive shop like Shopify. Shopify is even integrated with Oberlo, so you can create your account, pay your dues, and then all of the products you sign up to sell on Oberlo will appear in your Shopify. You can also use Amazon and eBay to post your drop shipping items.

Multi-Level Marketing (MLM)

An example of a multi-level marketing business would be Avon, which has been around since 1886! David H. McConnell was an unsuccessful book salesman who had a brilliant marketing idea. As an author, he gave away rose-scented perfume he made as a "free gift" to encourage people to buy his books.

You can use this same marketing tactic with pet supplies. Hopefully with as much success as David H. McConnell.

With MLM, you advertise your business and reach customers with samples. When a customer places an order, you order through your account with your retailer discount and have the product delivered to the customer. For every sale you make, you get a percentage commission. You also get money for signing up new retailers with your account.

Here are a few multi-level marketing companies that sell pet products (Resources):

- Life's Abundance sells pet food, cleaning products, and supplements for pets and humans.
- Pawtree sells pet beds, toys, treatments, supplements, food, and other products.
- NéVetica has a wide variety of training and cleaning products related to pets.
- HB Naturals sells natural products for flea and tick protection, itch relief, pet health, and CBD products for pain relief.

Do This First

To get started with an MLM pet company, first visit the company's website. See if you agree with their values and history and want to represent them. You may also find a representative in your area and sample or order a few products.

If you like the company, sign up with your area representative or sign up directly on the company's site if there are no representatives in your area. The company will probably have you purchase a starter kit and will provide you with catalogs, a website, and business cards.

Independent Shop

If you make your own pet products, you can sell them online through your own website.

For each product, post ample pictures. For instance, if you're making dog cookies, you need a high-quality photo of one of the cookies and a couple of the package—so users know what to expect. For extra advertising, show your dog enjoying the cookie to prove it's canine approved. If you're selling a pet bed, you will need to show it from all angles, including the measurements, and also show a pet enjoying it.

You want to be transparent about materials or ingredients. Since new customers don't know your products, they will have lots of questions. You can set their minds at ease by indicating exactly what is in your products—let pet lovers know what they're buying. You never know if a pet or its owner has allergies to your tasty pet treats!

Offering free samples can be a good way to get customers to

Do This First

To get started with an MLM pet company, first visit the company's website. See if you agree with their values and history and want to represent them. You may also find a representative in your area and sample or order a few products.

If you like the company, sign up with your area representative or sign up directly on the company's site if there are no representatives in your area. The company will probably have you purchase a starter kit and will provide you with catalogs, a website, and business cards.

Independent Shop

If you make your own pet products, you can sell them online through your own website.

For each product, post ample pictures. For instance, if you're making dog cookies, you need a high-quality photo of one of the cookies and a couple of the package—so users know what to expect. For extra advertising, show your dog enjoying the cookie to prove it's canine approved. If you're selling a pet bed, you will need to show it from all angles, including the measurements, and also show a pet enjoying it.

You want to be transparent about materials or ingredients. Since new customers don't know your products, they will have lots of questions. You can set their minds at ease by indicating exactly what is in your products—let pet lovers know what they're buying. You never know if a pet or its owner has allergies to your tasty pet treats!

Offering free samples can be a good way to get customers to

Multi-Level Marketing (MLM)

An example of a multi-level marketing business would be Avon, which has been around since 1886! David H. McConnell was an unsuccessful book salesman who had a brilliant marketing idea. As an author, he gave away rose-scented perfume he made as a "free gift" to encourage people to buy his books.

You can use this same marketing tactic with pet supplies. Hopefully with as much success as David H. McConnell.

With MLM, you advertise your business and reach customers with samples. When a customer places an order, you order through your account with your retailer discount and have the product delivered to the customer. For every sale you make, you get a percentage commission. You also get money for signing up new retailers with your account.

Here are a few multi-level marketing companies that sell pet products (Resources):

- Life's Abundance sells pet food, cleaning products, and supplements for pets and humans.
- Pawtree sells pet beds, toys, treatments, supplements, food, and other products.
- NéVetica has a wide variety of training and cleaning products related to pets.
- HB Naturals sells natural products for flea and tick protection, itch relief, pet health, and CBD products for pain relief.

buy your products. For instance, offer new customers a free bottle of your homemade dog shampoo or a small bag of cat treats along with any purchase. Hand out samples at local events, as well. The more people try your goods and like them, the more reviews you will get. Then your brand becomes trustworthy to total strangers.

Important Considerations

In the industry of selling pet products, you won't get to interact with pets. The main customers you deal with are human ones! You must offer superior customer service to get good reviews and repeat business. Your business will survive based on the good experiences and reviews of past customers.

Things can, and do, go wrong in these businesses. Maybe an order arrives damaged or doesn't arrive at all. Maybe a customer doesn't like the product. You must patiently address all problems. Make your return policy clear. Be prepared to absorb the cost of lost shipments.

If you are selling your own products, be prepared for people to have lots of questions. They don't know your product, so they can't trust it yet. You must build a great reputation and get as many reviews as you can.

Business will pick up in time. As you earn more and more good reviews, you can sell more and more. You may need to get a larger space for manufacturing and/or hire help to meet demand. Always post all ingredients in your products and answer any questions or concerns customers may have.

Expected Salary: up to $100,000 a year

Wrap-Up

As a pet lover, you want the best supplies for your customers' beloved companions. That's why creating an online pet product business is a lucrative way to enter the pet industry. Decide if you want to drop ship products from other manufacturers, sell your own products, or become part of a multi-level marketing organization.

For your customers to find you, and to help with sales, create a website featuring your goods and your company profile and begin marketing. You will enjoy becoming a trusted retailer for pet and animal lovers everywhere. You will also love working in your pajamas!

If running an online pet business is not what you want to do, then you can learn how to become an animal communicator in the next chapter. Animal communicators often work with animals and their owners to deliver intuitive messages to help solve health and behavioral issues. You will be a voice for pets everywhere!

But don't forget your action steps for this chapter. They will help you stay focused and determine if opening an online store is for you.

Action Steps

1. Decide what type of pet product business you want to run: drop shipping, independent selling, or multi-level marketing.
2. Start a website or Shopify account. You should also

create Amazon and/or eBay accounts, as these are popular platforms.
3. Build a brand. Represent something and tailor your marketing and products to the people most likely to buy them.
4. Use Amazon and Google Keyword Planner to find what sells.
5. Contact drop shipping businesses personally or on a marketplace to begin your business.
6. Sign up for an MLM organization. Go through a local representative if possible.
7. Post pictures and descriptions of your goods. Make them to order.
8. Offer superior customer service.
9. Go to the resource section of this book for helpful links.

3

ANIMAL COMMUNICATOR

Are you into the intuitive side of life? A lot of people would love to be able to hear what their pets are thinking. Our companions have a lot to say, and it is popular for people to hire communicators to interpret their silent, spiritual messages using telepathy (Glossary).

Some communicators communicate with live pets; others communicate with pets who have reached the end of their lives (animal medium). Either way, you will find many people clamoring for your services in the spiritual and mental realm of pet communication.

If you understand that animals speak without words, then you are already prepared to become an animal communicator. Many animals are angry and frustrated because their people don't realize how they are misunderstood. Some are disheartened by injuries or illnesses and need help voicing their needs; some see their people struggling with life issues and want to offer reassurance but can't.

3

ANIMAL COMMUNICATOR

Are you into the intuitive side of life? A lot of people would love to be able to hear what their pets are thinking. Our companions have a lot to say, and it is popular for people to hire communicators to interpret their silent, spiritual messages using telepathy (Glossary).

Some communicators communicate with live pets; others communicate with pets who have reached the end of their lives (animal medium). Either way, you will find many people clamoring for your services in the spiritual and mental realm of pet communication.

If you understand that animals speak without words, then you are already prepared to become an animal communicator. Many animals are angry and frustrated because their people don't realize how they are misunderstood. Some are disheartened by injuries or illnesses and need help voicing their needs; some see their people struggling with life issues and want to offer reassurance but can't.

create Amazon and/or eBay accounts, as these are popular platforms.
3. Build a brand. Represent something and tailor your marketing and products to the people most likely to buy them.
4. Use Amazon and Google Keyword Planner to find what sells.
5. Contact drop shipping businesses personally or on a marketplace to begin your business.
6. Sign up for an MLM organization. Go through a local representative if possible.
7. Post pictures and descriptions of your goods. Make them to order.
8. Offer superior customer service.
9. Go to the resource section of this book for helpful links.

You will listen to these animals carefully and understand their feelings by reading their body language and mental thoughts. Then you can translate these messages to their person and improve the relationship between the pet and human exponentially.

With some practice, you can begin to work with veterinarians and vet assistants, animal competitors, wildlife rescuers, zookeepers, and individual pet lovers. Before you become a trusted animal communicator, however, you need to go through some training. There is no formal school for animal communication; however, there are a variety of animal communication "certifications" available online. You can also learn a lot from a mentorship with a reputable animal communicator.

You must first find an animal communicator with a steady track record of working with animals professionally. Many professional animal communicators work with veterinarians, dog trainers, and various other professionals. You can also find them through an online search. When you do find someone that has credibility, politely approach the communicator and express an interest in learning the trade.

Your mentor can tell you about workshops where you learn to clear your mind to receive telepathic messages and other tools necessary to have a lucrative career. You will get hands-on practice working with animals. In addition to the workshop, you must practice with animals—starting with your own animals. Ask other pet peeps if you can practice with their pets and share the messages you receive to establish your reputation.

There are also institutes, often online, which teach animal

communication skills. Do not just sign up for any school. Research the school and see if its values align with your own. Also, look at its student reviews to find out if other people have had a good experience with the institute.

As you practice, you will establish a great reputation. When you feel ready to go pro, create a website and begin reaching out to businesses that may need your services. You can leave business cards at boarding kennels and veterinarian offices to reach owners who may want to communicate with their pets.

Be sure to network with animal lovers and people in the pet industry and show them what you can do by communicating briefly with their pets as a sort of "sample" of your services. As people see what you can do, they will eagerly hire you.

Business will naturally come to you, as people want to hear what their pets have to say. Once you become established, you may also consider mentoring new communicators or teaching classes to supplement your business.

You can work as a communicator online or in person. In the beginning, it is easier to meet animals in person. However, once you are proficient with your skills, you can often channel an animal's spirit online and conduct appointments via phone, email, or utilizing a face-to-face platform like Zoom or Skype.

Important Considerations

Animal communication is a rewarding career that can make all the difference in the lives of pets and their people. I have been an animal communicator for over forty years and have helped countless people understand their animals. I have also trained other animal communicators who have gone on to have successful and rewarding careers.

Keep in mind you may hear heart-wrenching stories from animals about abuse, neglect, pain, and troubled emotions. You may also encounter difficult owners and skeptics who doubt the validity of your career. Simply accept that you are doing your part to help pets for those who want help and you will be able to navigate these issues gracefully.

Expected Salary: $40,000-plus a year

Wrap-Up

You now have the basic information to consider a rewarding career by becoming a professional animal communicator. If you are able to clear your mind and receive telepathic messages from pets or if you have a fine eye for body language, you can help a lot of people and make a huge difference in their relationships with their pets.

As an animal communicator, you can work online or in person. Review the action steps in this chapter to find the training you need.

Animal communication is not for everyone. If you don't feel that this is the career for you, then read on to learn how to become a pet loss grief mentor. This career is especially beneficial for those with excellent empathy and listening skills—and a deep love for pets. You will be acting as a grief coach and support system for people going through shattering pet losses.

Action Steps

1. Download my free gift that has websites to get you started (https://wendyvandepoll.com/pet-jobs-free-gift).
2. Have an animal communication session done for you and your beloved companion to see if this is a career that interests you.
3. Find a good mentor who has great testimonials and track record.
4. Take a class to see if animal communication is for you.
5. Enroll in an institute or animal communication program that has a great reputation.
6. Practice, practice, practice.
7. Create your website, distribute business cards at local pet businesses, and network with people in the pet industry.

4

PET LOSS GRIEF MENTOR

Do you find yourself listening with compassion to people's stories after they have lost their companion? Most people love their pets like family. There is a reason we call our pets our fur babies! But sadly, our pets don't live as long as us. Many people are thrown into emotional tailspins after losing their furry loved ones.

Pet loss grief is a rewarding industry, but also an important and emotionally significant one. With pet loss grief mentoring, you can help heal the lives and hearts of pet owners who are going through tremendous suffering.

Pet loss grief mentoring is not unlike grief counseling. However, you do not have a licensed degree. I am a certified life coach with an extra certification for end-of-life and grief coaching. I follow the ethical code of being certified as a coach.

As a pet loss grief mentor, you are coaching people to heal

themselves and come to terms with loss. You are teaching coping skills for the whole family. Finally, you are coaching people on how to cherish the memories of their pets in their own special way.

As a pet loss grief coach for over twenty years, I love what I do. On my website, CenterForPetLossGrief.com, I offer best-selling books, products, courses, and informative blog articles to help people through the pain of losing a beloved pet.

I also offer products like personalized pet loss poems to help owners mourn their lost pets, and I offer animal mediumship (Glossary) to impart comforting messages from pets to their people.

I can say that while my career deals with very sad subject matter, I come away from my job every day feeling grateful that I am able to help so many people. The main element of my job is providing comfort and education to bereaved people so that they can start healing.

To enter this career, you must love animals and possess an ability for compassion and empathy. You must treat each client individually and address their unique needs. There is no one-size-fits-all approach to pet loss grief. As a mentor, you must not tell people how to cope or grieve. Instead, you must guide them to find their own way.

To get started, you want to learn about grief. You don't have to become professionally licensed, but you do want to become a certified coach educated on the grieving process.

You want to create a website that is very accessible to people. Show people how you can help them and what services you offer to guide them through this tough time. Always use

WENDY VAN DE POLL

of-life and grief coach, you will have to be professional and follow a code of ethics.

To decide if pet loss grief coaching or mentoring is for you, please go to the action steps. Make your lists and do your research. This is a rewarding profession, but you must be able to listen to people talk about their grief as well as take care of yourself so you don't suffer from compassion fatigue or burnout.

Next, if you have something important to teach other pet owners, please consider becoming an online course creator. Selling information online is a huge business these days. You can make a lot of money without ever leaving your computer chair with an online course.

Action Steps

1. Make a list that includes every reason why you want to become a pet loss grief mentor.
2. Once your list is completed, rate them from one to ten, with one being your top reason.
3. Make note if there are any points you listed that would concern you.
4. If not, start your research for coaching programs. You may have to go with basic life coaching first and then find a continuing education course for end-of-life training.
5. Once you are up and running, create your website, social media platforms, and start networking.
6. Download my free gift that has websites for additional support (Resources).

Important Considerations

Pet loss grief is certainly heart-wrenching. As you hear people share stories of their loss and their grief, your heart will go out to them. However, you can't let the sadness stop you from helping your clients. You will have to take care of yourself so you don't develop compassion fatigue and burnout.

Your job will deal with people more than animals. You will probably not work with animals in a hands-on capacity, unless you offer pet hospice work and become an animal energy practitioner (Chapter 14) or animal massage therapist (Chapter 16).

Expected Salary: 35,000–50,000 per year

Wrap-Up

Animal companions become a part of their people's hearts and souls—it is natural for people to feel devastated when they pass. It will be important, if you choose this profession, to manage your compassion fatigue to avoid burnout. I cover this a lot in my book, *The Pet Professional's Guide to Pet Loss Grief: How to Prevent Burnout, Support Clients, and Manage the Business of Grief.*

Many pet peeps struggle with grief when their animal companions reach the end of their lives. Thus, it is important to offer them guidance and support in this painful process.

There are many facets to this profession, and the most important is to get the proper training. Without proper training, there are risks. You could actually say the wrong thing and make your client feel worse. When becoming a certified end-

compassionate language and muted colors to instill a sense of comfort in your clients.

Create a blog and an online store for any pet loss grief-related products or courses you may offer. Courses and books are excellent products to sell on your site.

Any courses and books you offer should deal explicitly with matters pertaining to specific aspects of grieving. For instance, you might offer a course on how parents can help their children grieve pet loss, or you might offer a book on forgiving yourself for guilt related to a pet's demise.

You can also offer one-on-one support by acting as a mentor—listening and providing resources for people. You must remind them not to place timelines on their grief or feel badly about how their grieving process works.

Patience, compassion, and gentle comfort are essential. But so is honesty. You never want to lie to your clients, who come to rely on you for help navigating their new reality without their beloved companions.

Marketing includes many online channels. You can create a brand on social media that promotes your compassionate and helpful mission. By blogging and using many keywords, you can appear higher on search engine results when grieving pet owners turn to the Internet for resources. You may consider in-person advertising. You can ask pet cremation businesses and vet clinics to distribute your card to clients suffering from pet loss.

5

ONLINE COURSE CREATOR

Are you an educator, or would you like to become an educator? This is the Information Age. People are willing to pay money for information delivered in a palatable and convenient online format.

Being able to learn from home drives people to download courses on subjects they are interested in. Since there is a great deal to learn about animals, you can be very successful with an enlightening online school!

The first step is figuring out what you have to teach others. Maybe you can teach people how to properly potty-train a dog, or how to train a horse using a clicker.

If you are a cat lover or cat professional, you can teach people how to groom and bathe cats without tons of scratches. Delve into your mind, figure out what animal skills you can teach pet parents, and draw from that.

In my Spirit Paw Academy courses (Resources), I use my expertise in pet loss grief support and animal communication to help families who have lost pets cope and grieve. For a fee, people can purchase my courses and get support from me with the valuable information I offer. On my site, I market my courses by letting customers know how each course will help them.

That's why your second step is finding your target audience. Certain people will definitely want to learn what you know. A snake lover would love to learn how to handle his or her snake, while a dog person may not. So, figure out who wants to learn what you teach and then aim your course and your marketing at that group.

Social media is a handy research tool. Look into groups of pet parents in the niche you are teaching in. See the problems they often raise or the questions they commonly ask. Also, research other courses that are popular and observe how the instructor handles the problems and solutions of their potential students.

You want to mention these common problems in your course, but you also want to offer something different than the competition—find something unique to add to your course.

Once you have found your demographic and your course subject, you can begin crafting your course. There are many course platforms available, but my favorite is Teachable.com (Resources).

Here are some steps to begin crafting your course:

Your course needs to solve a problem for people. Once you determine the problem your course will cover, define the problem very clearly. My course solves the problem many people face of how to cope with grief after pet loss. For example: *Do you feel alone with your pet loss grief?*

Research the problem. Learn all you can about it and determine how common the problem is. Then draw from your own expertise. Your experience and any formal or professional training you may have makes you a more respected authority.

Create an outline. Group similar ideas into chapters or lessons. Decide how much time to dedicate to each topic based on importance. Cut out topics that don't fit into the overall subject of your course.

For instance, you could teach a course for dog peeps. A great class would be…Housetraining 101: How to Teach Your Dog to Ring a Bell to go Outside.

1. Class 1: Train your dog to touch the bell with their nose.
2. Class 2: Train your dog to ring the bell at the door(s).
3. Class 3: Train your dog when to ring the bell. Potty time only!

Decide how to present the information. Most people like videos the best, as they are the easiest to learn from. I like to present a combination of videos, written content, and slides to make the course most palatable. Presenting the information in a few ways ensures your students will absorb the information —since everyone has their own learning style.

Set a reasonable price for your course. Research what similar courses are selling for to help you find a reasonable amount.

Next, get it online. Offer it on your website and emphasize why people should buy it. Tell them how it will solve a problem for them. Run some type of special and offer a checklist or other lead magnet that divulges a small amount of information from the course. This entices people to buy the course to view the rest of the information and gain the full benefits you promise.

When people buy the course, you can send the material all at once, or Teachable allows you to "drip" the content in periodic increments. I like the drip method the best because then people can digest the information and give themselves time to do the action steps I created for them.

Important Considerations

A course is a way to earn income after you perform the initial work of setting it up. All you have to do is market it and get people to sign up for it. However, the initial work can be quite time-consuming and challenging. Take your time and seek help when you need it.

You also need to provide people with support if they have trouble with your course. People might have questions, or they might say your course didn't work for them. You have to help them by providing answers to their issues.

Expected Salary: varies depending on your niche and how much work you put into marketing.

Wrap-Up

Creating an online course is a fun way to educate people about an important issue and help solve their problems. If your course solves a problem for people, then it is instantly marketable. You just have to promote it and prove to people how it is helpful.

There are many steps when it comes to creating a course, and this chapter helped you get started. When you are brainstorming your course, keep in mind to create content that is unique and helpful. Offer realistic tips and tools to help your students be successful.

Visit the action steps to keep you on task if you want to try developing a course. Check out the options with Teachable.com as a host platform, and have fun. Course creation is one of my favorites.

If you are artistic and love animals, you're going to love the career choice in Chapter 6. Read on to learn how to combine art and the pet industry into one by becoming a pet portrait artist!

Action Steps

1. Ask your following some issues they may be struggling with.
2. If you don't have a following, do some Google searches to see what other online courses offer and look like.

3. Choose your platform to host your course. I like Teachable.
4. Brainstorm your course material around said problem and figure out a unique way to solve the issue.
5. Create the content. Consider video, slides, audio, and PDF downloads.
6. Price it according to your market research.
7. Market! Market! Market!

6

PET PORTRAIT ARTIST

Are you an artist and in love with animals? Many people love their pets more than life itself. They love to memorialize and honor their pets with portraits. You can create a unique portrait via a medium you enjoy and put your artistic skills to monetized use.

I have seen pet portraits run as high as $10,000! This isn't the norm for this industry, but you can do the research to see what is appropriate for your skill level. You can set your price and potentially make a decent salary.

There are a few mediums to choose from when creating a pet portrait. You can draw using pencils, paint with watercolor, oils, or acrylics, or use pastels and charcoal.

You can even create computer animations or digitized pictures of people's beloved companions. Having your own unique look will make people seek you out. They will want one of *your* portraits—not just any portrait. For even more profit, you can incorporate a variety of mediums and styles to match the tastes of even more pet people.

Start by creating a few winning portraits of your own pets or the pets of your friends. Post these on a portfolio page on your website. Then, start posting your work on social media, especially in a variety of animal groups. Also, pay for social media advertising that places your ad in front of people who have searched for pet portrait artists.

Next, visit local pet and art businesses and leave behind your business cards. Network at events, like dog shows or trade shows, and hand out business cards there as well. You can set up a booth at local events that allow art vendors, particularly art festivals and craft fairs, and hang your art to attract interested customers.

Also consider creating a profile on Etsy and offering custom portrait services. Etsy is a place where many people go to find art, so you can reach many customers there. Have people send you pictures of their pets or arrange to meet in person so that you can begin the portrait.

Important Considerations

Your success as a pet portrait artist goes far beyond having artistic skills. Delivering art to customers on time, being gentle with pets, and displaying great customer service skills will make you a favored artist in the pet community.

Keep in mind people involved with animal groups and events are extremely loyal to each other. Always be aware of building your career with meticulous professionalism. People network, and when you are good at what you do and exercise profes-

you can incorporate a variety of mediums and styles to match the tastes of even more pet people.

Start by creating a few winning portraits of your own pets or the pets of your friends. Post these on a portfolio page on your website. Then, start posting your work on social media, especially in a variety of animal groups. Also, pay for social media advertising that places your ad in front of people who have searched for pet portrait artists.

Next, visit local pet and art businesses and leave behind your business cards. Network at events, like dog shows or trade shows, and hand out business cards there as well. You can set up a booth at local events that allow art vendors, particularly art festivals and craft fairs, and hang your art to attract interested customers.

Also consider creating a profile on Etsy and offering custom portrait services. Etsy is a place where many people go to find art, so you can reach many customers there. Have people send you pictures of their pets or arrange to meet in person so that you can begin the portrait.

Important Considerations

Your success as a pet portrait artist goes far beyond having artistic skills. Delivering art to customers on time, being gentle with pets, and displaying great customer service skills will make you a favored artist in the pet community.

Keep in mind people involved with animal groups and events are extremely loyal to each other. Always be aware of building your career with meticulous professionalism. People network, and when you are good at what you do and exercise profes-

6

PET PORTRAIT ARTIST

Are you an artist and in love with animals? Many people love their pets more than life itself. They love to memorialize and honor their pets with portraits. You can create a unique portrait via a medium you enjoy and put your artistic skills to monetized use.

I have seen pet portraits run as high as $10,000! This isn't the norm for this industry, but you can do the research to see what is appropriate for your skill level. You can set your price and potentially make a decent salary.

There are a few mediums to choose from when creating a pet portrait. You can draw using pencils, paint with watercolor, oils, or acrylics, or use pastels and charcoal.

You can even create computer animations or digitized pictures of people's beloved companions. Having your own unique look will make people seek you out. They will want one of *your* portraits—not just any portrait. For even more profit,

sionalism, people will recommend you. You want to make a great impression and earn lots of great reviews.

Also consider how to present your artwork. You must invest in a lovely portfolio that displays your work in good lighting, with proper pixilation. Create your website and portfolio to look professional and beautiful (Chapters 30 and 31). As you finish new portraits, be sure to update your portfolio. A robust portfolio will give people a better sense of your work and convince them to hire you.

As a pet portrait artist, you can work online using photographs of pets that owners send you. Or you can work in person and meet the pets to decide how you are going to capture their personalities.

Expected Salary: $35,000–$40,000 a year

Wrap-Up

If you love painting and drawing, you can certainly make many pet peeps happy with lovely portraits of their pets. Using your own medium and artistic expression, you can create an attractive brand people will recognize.

Networking is important. Be ready to attend art events, dog and cat shows, and other pet events to gain notoriety. Also join various Facebook groups where your services may be of interest to the members of the group.

Your artwork will sell itself as long as you are professional and have skill. You can work from home using photos or meet pets in person, but a majority of your marketing will take place online.

The action steps in this chapter will remind you what needs to be done in order to be a successful pet portrait artist. Write these action steps on a postcard and hang it where you can see it as you build your business.

For another career involving art and pets, read on to the next chapter and learn how to become a pet T-shirt designer.

Action Steps

1. Create pet portraits of your own pets and post it in an online portfolio to get started.
2. Hand out business cards and have booths at craft fairs and local events.
3. Open a shop on Etsy and advertise your store using social media.
4. Blast your art on social media and pay for social media advertising.
5. Deliver professional customer service to gain loyal followers.

7

PET T-SHIRT DESIGNER

Do you have a love for design, T-shirts, and animals? Like pet portraits, you can design shirts that let people celebrate their close relationships with their pets and animals in general. There is definitely a market for T-shirts with great quotes and art involving animals.

There are a variety of ways you can open a T-shirt business. Some people hire printing companies to mass produce the clothes with a specific print they design. Others make the shirts themselves, which does take more time and money but also fetches a higher price per article of clothing. Amazon also has a program for T-shirt designers that is excellent.

To begin, you should have some artistic ability in order to sketch your designs. You need to learn how to use Adobe Photoshop and Illustrator to create your sketches on the computer. There are free courses on Udemy for how to use this software.

From there, you need to practice! Some people go to school for graphic design, but school is not truly necessary. You can teach yourself the skills you need and build a portfolio!

When you have a portfolio, be sure to post it online. Show off your work. Show off a few designs that have done well so that people can order them. If a design doesn't sell well, scrap it and replace it with a new design. Then test how it sells. You don't want your shop full of designs no one orders.

Offer a few options of T-shirt styles, such as V-neck and crew neck. Also offer a couple color options. If your business does well, you can expand it to include mugs, wallets, phone cases, bedding, calendars, and other types of printing.

Reach out to people in your area and offer to make free T-shirts. Ask local businesses, like pet supply stores, if they would like to have T-shirts made. Make some T-shirts for a local shelter. As you expand your portfolio and learn the trade, you will be able to eventually sell your shirts.

When you hear about local craft fairs or vendor events, set up a booth and display your T-shirts as well as a printed portfolio of all of your designs. This gets the word out about your online business and also helps you make sales in person. Finally, look into clothing shows where you can represent yourself as a designer.

Important Considerations

T-shirt design is fun and promotes great work-life balance. You can work when you want. You can also create your own design studio and printing shop in your home and avoid needing warehouse space by creating T-shirts to order. Or you can sign up with Amazon's T-shirt business.

It you print at home, the start-up costs can be high. To print T-shirts on your own, you are looking at up to $50,000 for all of the computers and printing equipment. It is far easier to find a local printer and have them print your shirts, usually for a few hundred dollars—depending on the number of shirts you order.

Along with Amazon, there are a few other online options, such as Shutterfly, Rush Order Tees, and Stitch Fix (Resources). Only order a few T-shirts at the start to present your work, and then order them as customers order them. Factor the cost of the printing into the price you charge customers.

Have local businesses carry your T-shirts on consignment, and don't forget to advertise on Facebook, Instagram, and Etsy.

Expected Salary: $39,000 a year

Wrap-Up

As an artist, you can create amazing pet-themed designs and custom prints for T-shirts and other printed material. Since people love to celebrate their pets, they are eager to buy prints featuring their animals.

There are different options for your T-shirt business, from opening your own printing shop to having a shop on Amazon. Do the research needed to determine what fits your lifestyle and budget.

T-shirt printing can have high start-up costs—be prepared. Most of your business will be online, but you can also sell your shirts locally and at vendor events. Be prepared to do a lot of marketing to get your shop up and running.

Before you go on to Chapter 8 to learn about becoming a pet brand creator, review the action steps below to see if opening a T-shirt business is a good fit for you.

Action Steps

1. Research Amazon, Etsy, and other platforms where you can host your T-shirt business.
2. Learn Adobe Photoshop and Illustrator. Practice drawing on the computer.
3. Approach local businesses and offer to print shirts for them for free. Gain practice and market yourself this way. Design the shirts and then print them locally or online to save money.
4. Take pictures of your shirts and your designs and put them on a portfolio page on your website.
5. Advertise on social media.
6. Go to local events, use local businesses, and attend clothing trade shows to get your name out there and make sales.

8

PET BRAND CREATOR

Some folks in the pet industry may be looking for someone to help them create their unique brand. They don't have the desire, knowledge, or time to spend on designing their logo, website, social media platforms, etc.

If you are interested in this career, you must have training in order to create successful businesses for other people. A degree in business with an emphasis on branding (Glossary) is recommended.

If you search the Internet, you will find a plethora of branding coaches that offer all types of services to help people create profitable businesses. My favorite is Donald Miller of StoryBrand.

Creating a pet brand is as simple as creating a name that people know and trust. You encompass certain qualities and values other people can relate to. This makes people buy the brand exclusively and trust the brand fully. As a brand creator, your job is to help people in the pet industry create this special name and following for their pet businesses. You might work with veterinarian clinics, dog food makers, groomers, rescue groups—anyone and anything pet!

A pet brand can include any pet-related business, ranging from delightful podcasts about raising puppies to informational courses that help people with their reptiles to compassionate pet cremation and burial services.

You will help a person create a website, social media sites, blog entries, pictures, a catalog, and more to generate their brand. You may also help someone with customer service and damage control when their brands are threatened by market changes, irate customers, and other such things.

A great pet brand simply taps into the love and compassion people feel for animals. If you prove that your client embodies those values with their products, blogs, or services, then you will be successful.

For each client, you want to find his or her voice, values, and a way to represent that in an appealing way. You will create a story, a mission statement, and even a logo and website to show the brand's heart and soul.

Your main costs will involve your website and any social media advertising you use. Start by determining what services you plan to offer. Some brand creators offer web design, while others focus on writing web content and blogging.

The more services you can offer, the more money you will make. You can brush up on web design skills, writing skills, social media management, and photography skills to help you become successful at this business. Many of these skills are offered online or through community colleges.

Then set your rates. Most brand creators charge by the hour, but some charge by the service. Rates vary, so research your region and what other pet brand professionals charge.

Next, do some work for a local pet shelter or other business. Get written permission to share what you do for that business in a portfolio. You only need two to three great jobs to showcase your skills. Post them on social media and your website to gain attention.

Be sure to reach out to new businesses with your card, inviting them to look at your portfolio. You can contact new online businesses and post your services on sites like Fiverr. As you begin to get clients, work to build a great reputation and earn great reviews, as clients will be your best source of free advertisement.

When you land a client, you must be very open. Make your services very transparent and be honest about your availability and how long it will take to complete a task. Don't promise your client that you will have his or her brand built in two days and then do a rush job or let them down! If your client wants a big project done in two weeks, be honest and say you can't do it.

Be sure to interview the client in person or over the phone. Ask many questions about what he or she is expecting so that you can deliver. Learn about his or her backstory, experience with pets, mission, vision, and more. As you work for the client, try to capture all of this. Always submit work for the client's review before you post it online to ensure that you are meeting the client's expectations.

Important Considerations

Creating a brand in the pet world is fairly easy, since pet lovers will readily identify with any brand that caters to pets and includes cute animal photos. To keep faithful clients, get to know them and their audiences well. Give them a unique voice and look. Always stick to the same format for any future work you do for them, as brands must stay reliable.

If a brand is not doing well, adjustments are in order. You have to be able to criticize your own work and see what is not working. You must also take criticism from your clients, who may want many tweaks and edits.

You may deal with irrational or vague clients. Clear communication is in order. Get to know a client well and ask lots of questions to capture their voice. You may have to make last-minute adjustments, which can be aggravating.

Expected Salary: $42,400–$92,000 a year

Wrap-Up

Creating a brand in the pet world is fairly easy, since pet lovers will readily identify with any brand that caters to their needs.

To keep faithful clients, get to know them and their audiences very well. Give them a unique voice and look. Always stick to the same format for any future work you do for them, as brands must stay reliable.

If a brand is not doing well, adjustments are in order. You have to be able to criticize your own work and see what is not working. You must also take criticism from your clients, who may want many tweaks and edits.

You may deal with irrational or vague clients. Clear communication is in order. Get to know a client well and ask lots of questions to capture their voice. You may have to make last-minute adjustments, which can be aggravating.

The action steps below will help you decide if becoming a pet brand creator is for you.

In this next section, you are going to learn all about pet businesses that require in-person interaction with pets and owners. These careers are both fun and challenging in their own ways, so you must enter these careers informed. The following chapters will teach you everything you need to know about starting and succeeding in these businesses.

Action Steps

1. Decide what services you will offer (website design, photography, blogging, social media management, logo creation, etc.).
2. Get some experience providing these services for free to places like animal shelters to gain experience and grow a portfolio.
3. Create a website with an aesthetic that you think people will find appealing. Post some of your work.
4. Interview clients thoroughly.

5. Send them content and have them review websites or blog posts before you post them.
6. Have your clients engage with followers on social media or have them hire social media managers.
7. Make improvements as needed, but never perform any drastic changes that will make people lose faith in the stability of each brand.

5. Send them content and have them review websites or blog posts before you post them.
6. Have your clients engage with followers on social media or have them hire social media managers.
7. Make improvements as needed, but never perform any drastic changes that will make people lose faith in the stability of each brand.

If a brand is not doing well, adjustments are in order. You have to be able to criticize your own work and see what is not working. You must also take criticism from your clients, who may want many tweaks and edits.

You may deal with irrational or vague clients. Clear communication is in order. Get to know a client well and ask lots of questions to capture their voice. You may have to make last-minute adjustments, which can be aggravating.

The action steps below will help you decide if becoming a pet brand creator is for you.

In this next section, you are going to learn all about pet businesses that require in-person interaction with pets and owners. These careers are both fun and challenging in their own ways, so you must enter these careers informed. The following chapters will teach you everything you need to know about starting and succeeding in these businesses.

Action Steps

1. Decide what services you will offer (website design, photography, blogging, social media management, logo creation, etc.).
2. Get some experience providing these services for free to places like animal shelters to gain experience and grow a portfolio.
3. Create a website with an aesthetic that you think people will find appealing. Post some of your work.
4. Interview clients thoroughly.

SECTION II

IN PERSON PET JOBS

Would you rather work with animals face-to-face? This section is all about learning how to make a career out of caring for or working with pets in person. Remember, a website and some online work is still necessary to advertise your services.

This section is for those who want to primarily do hands-on work with animals. There are many choices for in-person pet businesses. It just takes some time to figure out which one is for you.

9

PET PHOTOGRAPHER

Don't you just love pictures of adorable kittens and sweet puppies? Of course you do! That is why you can make a profitable living as a pet photographer. Not only can you be a photographer for pet peeps and take portraits of their beloved pets—you can also submit your photos for calendars, catalogs, stock photo sites, and magazines.

You can work for a company, or you can work independently. All you need is a website, professional camera, and a space for taking photos. It is also important to have the skills to work with all types of animals that have a variety of behaviors to get the perfect shot.

Start by getting a quality camera. You can browse professional photographer sites and forums to learn what you should buy. I won't discuss camera specifics here, since the camera industry is always changing. Take a few classes or skill courses to learn about lighting, pet posing, and how to use your camera. You should also get familiar with Adobe Photoshop and Illustrator, since a large part of photography entails editing pictures.

Next, practice. Do a few shoots for free to get the hang of it. You might volunteer to take photos at a shelter or have your friends bring their dogs by for photos. Try taking photos of your own pets. Use the best pictures in a portfolio that you post online and on your social media to prove your talent. Be sure to add watermarks or copyright images so that people don't copy and paste your work for free.

Create a website and business cards. You can use social media to advertise your photography. You can also hand out cards at local pet businesses and events. Be sure to include your best photo on the business card to give people a glimpse of your talent. Include your website address with your winning portfolio.

Offer your customers a few different options for print sizes. You might consider selling them engravings, T-shirts (Chapter 7), or things like mugs and calendars with their pets' photos. Have an entire catalog of products that you offer with the photos you take.

Important Considerations

Pet photography is a great business, and you can make hundreds of dollars a day shooting for a few hours. However, you must get used to demanding owners and pets who won't sit still for long and/or won't look at the camera. You may also encounter nervous pets who are prone to biting or scratching in fear.

Taking and editing great photos is a skill you need if you want to be successful. Consider taking a few courses on lighting, composition, setup, and handling animals.

Always be patient with the pet you are working with. Never force a pose or behavior. Some of the best shots of pets are candid and unplanned.

It is important—and a good business practice—to explain to the client you can't guarantee the client's desired image because animals don't always cooperate. This sets reasonable expectations for the client.

Expected Salary: $36,634-plus a year

Wrap-Up

You can take beautiful or cute pictures of pets for good money! The initial investment in a camera, Photoshop, and studio space can run up to a few thousand dollars, but it is definitely worth it. As you learn how to take photos of pets and work with pets and their owners, you will get even better and develop a magnificent portfolio.

There is a learning curve with pet photography, and it isn't just about taking great photos. It is important to, first and foremost, respect the needs of the animal. Learning how to naturally work with your subject will yield beautiful photos, but patience is needed.

The action steps in this chapter outline the basics of what you need to get started. Always remember to do your research to learn as much as you can about your chosen career.

In the next chapter, I talk about becoming a pet sitter. Taking care of people's pets is a huge industry and one that can be successful. Pet sitting is a valuable service that gives owners peace of mind while they are away.

Action Steps

1. Get a camera and take some courses in photography skills and pet photography.
2. Research what other pet photographers have on their websites and their specialties.
3. Practice and build a portfolio. Post your portfolio on your website.
4. Print cards with your website and best photo to distribute at stores and events.
5. Offer prints to your clients for an additional charge. Sell prints of images you own online as well.

10

PROFESSIONAL PET SITTER

Are you available on weekends and holidays when people go out of town? If so, a professional pet sitter is a great choice for a career. When people travel, they want someone they can trust to take care of their beloved non-human family members. As a pet sitter, you take on enormous responsibility. But you also make great money, have fun with pets, and give owners precious peace of mind. A rewarding career, professional pet sitting is a great way to work with animals in an unconventional setting.

Most pet sitters visit the owner's home for drop-in visits. They may stop by to take care of pets while the owner is on vacation, or they may drop in to walk dogs while the owner is at work. Others stay overnight, which is especially common for older pets or pets with special needs.

Pet sitters give animals the love, care, and attention they need while their owners are away in the comfort of their home settings. By doing drop-ins, you don't need to set up your own facility, but you do need a reliable car and phone.

Pet owners are placing a lot of trust in you by giving you a key to their homes and access to their cherished pets, so part of your job is proving that you deserve that trust.

To start, get the appropriate training and become a certified pet sitter. After your training, create a website and business cards that list your services and rates.

You can enroll on a site like Rover, which creates a profile and does some marketing for you. Advertise by leaving your cards at local pet businesses so pet peeps learn about you. If you want to provide drop-ins for busy professionals, try to approach people at business networking events and hand out business cards.

When working with a client, be sure to take lots of pictures of the pets you are caring for and send them to your client. Also be sure to learn the pet's feeding regimen and special needs—adhere to these things carefully. Let owners know what you have done with the pet after each drop-in visit with lots of photos. This reassures your client you are doing your job well and their companions are happy and safe.

Appreciative owners will likely tip you. Always urge them to leave you great reviews on Yelp, your personal website, and Rover. Good reviews will help you bring in more business. Ask the owner's permission to post photos of their pets enjoying their time with you on your site to bring in yet more trusting clients.

Important Considerations

You can expect to work on holidays and weekends. You will probably get more business over the summer than the winter, since people like to take vacations during the warmer months. This means that you may have to work on holidays and limit your vacations to slow times.

While pet sitting is a lucrative business, there are going to be lulls and slower months. When gas prices rise, people travel less—and you can expect less business. Be prepared for these fluctuations.

Pet sitting is a huge responsibility, and things can go wrong. A dog may run away while you are walking. A cat may get sick. You must plan for these issues and always take great care to avoid them.

If something does happen, your best course of action is to immediately alert the owner and be honest. The owner may be able to help you figure out how to solve the problem. Always have an emergency vet's number in your phone, as well.

Expected Salary: $48,635 a year, but varies

Wrap-Up

Pet sitting is a great way to interact directly with animals and give owners peace of mind while they are away. But things can go wrong, so take extra measures to prevent problems and remain calm when problems arise.

Make sure you get the training you need to become certified from one of the organizations I recommend in the resource section of this book. There are many aspects of pet sitting that are important to learn, and by being certified, you are providing the best care for your clients.

Pet sitting is a rewarding career, but plenty of work is involved. You must be available and enjoy working on weekends and on holidays. The room for building your business potential is huge with this career.

Refer to the action steps in this chapter if you choose this career. They will help you stay focused on what is important when starting your business and gaining clientele.

In the next chapter, you will learn how to become a dog trainer! Dog training allows you to improve relationships between dogs and their people. Dog training is a rewarding career if you love to teach.

Action Steps

1. Download my free gift that include websites to get you started (https://wendyvandepoll.com/pet-jobs-free-gift).
2. Choose a certification course and begin your training.
3. Create a website or Rover site and print your business cards.
4. Attend business network meetings. Leave your cards at local pet businesses.
5. As you drop in on pets, send owners updates with pictures.
6. Always adhere to a pet's feeding and medication

schedule. Feed the pet food he or she is used to. You want to avoid digestive upset.
7. Have an emergency vet's number on your phone.
8. If something goes wrong, notify the owner right away.
9. Urge people to leave you good reviews. With their permission, post photos of their happy pets on your site.

11

DOG TRAINER

Do you enjoy well-behaved dogs? Training dogs is extremely rewarding. You can help people and their pets have better relationships, help rescue dogs transition into new homes, and feel as if you made a difference in someone's life.

But there is more to being a dog trainer than simply teaching a dog to sit and stay. Dog trainers provide wonderful resources for people who are frustrated with their dogs' behavior, and they help improve relationships between dogs and their people. Furthermore, a dog trainer's job may entail preparing dogs for careers, such as bomb or drug sniffing, tracking, or showing and competing.

Typically, you want to get started by choosing the field you want to train in. If you are just getting started, I would suggest basic obedience skills. However, ask yourself these questions to determine your long-term goal:

- Do you want to train dogs on basic obedience and

provide people with tips on teaching a dog to be a good canine citizen?
- Do you want to teach a dog how to compete for show, agility, or some other sport?
- Do you want to train dogs for certain canine careers?
- Do you want to work with dogs used in movies?

There are many options! The one you choose depends on the difference you want to make in the dog world and your passion.

Next, you want to learn the ins and outs of dog training. Dog training is not as simple as professional trainers make it look! You have to learn how to work with dogs, read their body language, control your body language, understand animal behavior, and provide appropriate cues and rewards.

You can get training from a variety of schools. Some courses are in person, while others are online, or some combination of the two. I believe that hands-on, in-person training is ideal. The Certification Council for Professional Dog Trainers has a list of resources to help you find schools. You will find the URL when you download your free gift (https://wendyvandepoll.com/pet-jobs-free-gift).

It is often helpful to work with a mentor. Find a trainer in your desired field and work with him or her closely for at least a few months. Hands-on experience is an excellent companion to your written studies. Furthermore, you can find shelters looking for trainers or apprenticeships at training facilities. Look into dog training apprenticeships in your area or have your mentor help you find one.

Finally, you must get certified. A certification convinces pet owners that you know what you are doing, so you get more business. The Certification Council for Professional Dog Trainers is one place where you can get a trusted certification.

As you gain experience, you can start to advertise your business. Start with a website and distribute local flyers. Networking with other trainers and dog owners can help you gain loyal clients.

Important Considerations

Being a dog trainer is a valuable and lucrative career that can earn you up to $150 an hour—maybe more when you specialize. However, you must uphold ethical values and please both dogs and their owners with exceptional customer service.

It is essential you stay level-headed and never get frustrated, even if a dog or owner is difficult to work with. You may encounter scared, aggressive dogs, and you must handle the dog appropriately to minimize the risk of injury to yourself. Any dog training course will offer training on how to mitigate these risks.

Certification is an absolute must in order to be considered professional and trustworthy.

Expected Salary: $30,077-plus a year

Wrap-Up

If you want to train dogs, you can make a lot of money, have a lot of fun, and provide a valuable service for animals and their people.

Becoming a dog trainer is not an overnight career choice. There is certification to consider, apprenticeship opportunities, and building your business with time-tested approaches. You must also consider what type of dog training you want to do, as I outlined in this chapter.

Next, if you like working with pets and don't mind getting a little dirty, this career may be the one for you. But first take a look at the action steps at the end of this chapter.

If you are interested in making animals look sharp, read on to learn about how to become a groomer! Groomers can make excellent money while working directly with animals.

Action Steps

1. Download your free gift that includes schools and licensing bodies for dog training (https://wendyvandepoll.com/pet-jobs-free-gift).
2. Attend a certification course and get certified.
3. Find a mentor who is aligned with your principles.
4. Gain experience with this mentor and/or volunteer at shelters or rescue groups.
5. After you are certified and have established your business network, market yourself online and in person.
6. Always uphold customer service and ethical values in your training business.

12

GROOMER

Do you find satisfaction when creating something beautiful but don't mind hard work? Becoming a dog groomer may seem easy until you actually try to groom a dog! There is a large variety of cuts, hair types, and doggo dispositions that make this career interesting and unpredictable. You must learn how to groom dogs the right way, usually through a certification or apprenticeship program.

You may start by researching various certifications for dog grooming. I have a list for you when you download your free gift (https://wendyvandepoll.com/pet-jobs-free-gift). Proper certifications will expose you to a huge variety of types of dog hair and cuts, giving you valuable knowledge and experience. Plus, give you the training on how to start your business.

Another option that I don't recommend (because I'm all about certifications) is to approach a groomer in your area and express interest in training. The groomer may offer you an apprenticeship or refer you to a training program. Some groomers may hire you to wash dogs, and you can gain experience by watching how they work with and groom animals.

After your program, you can join The National Dog Groomers Association of America (Download Your Free Gift for the link), which is probably the most respected body for grooming certification. To get this certification, you must complete five tests over a five-year period and complete a course with the association.

There are a few other organizations that give certifications as well. Look into the one that fits your needs the most. You don't have to have a certification to groom animals, but it certainly helps boost your credibility, professionalism, and earning potential!

After your course, you should gain experience. Either offer services at low prices or work for a company to build a portfolio. You can also volunteer as a groomer for a shelter to gain necessary experience and help animals get adopted.

When you have some experience, glowing reviews, and a portfolio showing off at least five successful grooming jobs—create a website and start trying to draw in your own clients. You can advertise locally and online. You can also start your own shop or set up a grooming shop in your home when you believe you can get enough clients to justify the start-up costs.

Important Considerations

You are likely to encounter scared animals who will bite. Then there will be those difficult clients who demand perfection.

Because you will be working with animals, you will be exposed to fleas, ticks, skin conditions, and other challenging issues, including neglect.

To be successful in this profession, you must have a patient personality. Be able to soothe not only the animal but deal with challenging people. This career is a rewarding one, but it is not easy.

If you choose this profession, consider learning an energy technique (Chapter 14) or animal massage therapy (Chapter 16). They are great additions to your tool box and will help calm the animals you work on.

Also, you must keep your shop clean to not spread disease or parasites. Most groomers require proof of vaccinations before a client books with them to reduce the risk of spreading communicable diseases and parasites.

You can set your own policies if you have your own grooming business, but take as many precautions as you can. Always adhere to safe grooming and nail-trimming practices. If you do—you will succeed.

Expected Salary: $23,000-plus a year

Wrap-Up

Grooming is a fantastic way to work directly with animals. Once you are certified, you can continue with your education to include animal energy techniques, pet massage, or even specialize in cuts for show dogs.

With affordable education and start-up costs, you can have a career with a mid-range income. Certification, although not necessary—but recommended, gives you credibility, professionalism, and the business training needed to succeed.

Always take steps to keep your facility clean and free of parasites and diseases. Learn how to handle animals to prevent bites and scratches. Refer to the action steps to help guide you with this career choice.

If you are interested in making delectable treats for pets, then the next chapter is for you! Read on to learn how to start a pet bakery.

Action Steps

1. Find a training course that is respected. Do your homework on this one because not all training courses are comprehensive.
2. Download your free gift for a list of schools and certifications.
3. Get certified. Although not necessary, I highly suggest this option. You will appear more professional —which helps with business building practices.
4. Work for a company or volunteer at shelters to build a portfolio. This step is necessary when building a business.
5. Purchase equipment and a space, or set up in your home. You don't need much, but when you are starting out, you will need a few pieces. When you work from home, you can save on rent and deduct the space from your taxes.

6. Advertise your business. Even though word-of-mouth is the best advertising, you must do more. Join local business groups and network. Post your business cards around town and talk with other pet professionals to gain business.

6. Advertise your business. Even though word-of-mouth is the best advertising, you must do more. Join local business groups and network. Post your business cards around town and talk with other pet professionals to gain business.

career with a mid-range income. Certification, although not necessary—but recommended, gives you credibility, professionalism, and the business training needed to succeed.

Always take steps to keep your facility clean and free of parasites and diseases. Learn how to handle animals to prevent bites and scratches. Refer to the action steps to help guide you with this career choice.

If you are interested in making delectable treats for pets, then the next chapter is for you! Read on to learn how to start a pet bakery.

Action Steps

1. Find a training course that is respected. Do your homework on this one because not all training courses are comprehensive.
2. Download your free gift for a list of schools and certifications.
3. Get certified. Although not necessary, I highly suggest this option. You will appear more professional —which helps with business building practices.
4. Work for a company or volunteer at shelters to build a portfolio. This step is necessary when building a business.
5. Purchase equipment and a space, or set up in your home. You don't need much, but when you are starting out, you will need a few pieces. When you work from home, you can save on rent and deduct the space from your taxes.

need to speak to your city about applicable licenses. You may also have to register your business for tax purposes.

Anyone can create pet treats. That's why you must stand out from the competition and make owners feel that they should spend money at your bakery as opposed to buying a box of cheap pet treats made or sourced in China.

Offer something people love:

- Organic non-GMO ingredients.
- A special herbal blend that is safe for pets.
- Pet treats baked into cute shapes and frosted, as well as superior taste.

Find free recipes online and then try to make them unique, while always ensuring they are safe for the pet they are intended for!

I believe human-grade and natural ingredients should go into all pet treats and pet foods. If your human customers can eat it, then they will be more likely to feel good about feeding it to their pets. Be sure to use your packaging as advertising by sharing how you don't use preservatives, your treats are baked from the heart, you use organic ingredients, and so on.

Always advertise how your product is nutritious and healthy. This will be your main selling point. But presentation also matters, so making treats that look cute and palatable will work best for your business. Using catchy names for treats and creating holiday-themed treats and gift baskets will also boost sales.

13

PET BAKERY

As a pet lover, do you like to give your companions delicious, natural, and healthy treats? I make my own, so I know exactly what is going into what I am feeding them. If you love to bake and provide healthy treats for animals, you can make a decent living and warm many hearts by opening a pet bakery.

The great thing about opening a pet bakery is you can work out of your home or open a store. You can sell your treats online or in person. You can approach local pet businesses to carry your treats on consignment, too.

You can run your business out of your home and use something like Square and PayPal for credit card payments. Your start-up costs will only be a few hundred dollars or less for ingredients and baking supplies.

The best part is that you don't have to meet the same FDA and state standards as bakeries for humans! However, you may still

This can be a fun career choice if you love baking and don't mind the networking needed to get your treats bought and to gain loyal customers.

Next, in Chapter 14, learn how working with animals and their energy can provide healing for a variety of physical and emotional issues. I will share how you can become an animal energy practitioner.

Action Steps

1. Do your research by contacting your town offices to determine if you need licensing to open a pet bakery. Laws and restrictions will vary.
2. Choose where you will run your business—home, your own storefront, consignment space in a pet supply store.
3. This is the fun part. Research, develop, and taste your recipes before offering them for sale.
4. Make sure you purchase the supplies you need and your ingredients. Look for wholesale distributers so you can buy at a lower cost. I love Frontier Coop Wholesale (Resources).
5. Design your packaging to reflect your brand.
6. Create a beautiful and engaging website to entice your customers to buy your treats.
7. Make sure you follow trends. Offer holiday themes and gift baskets for your customers.
8. Download your free gift that has a list of contacts to start your business (Resources).

Important Considerations

Pet treats are adored by everyone, but you must market yourself by providing something better than the competition. Be sure to follow trends. Social media or trips to other successful pet bakeries can help you stay on top of trends.

A store that is dedicated solely to being a pet bakery may not thrive in a small community, so consider combining your bakery with another type of pet business if you are opening a store. While you can make a full-time career out of baking pet food and treats, this is more likely to be a successful side business.

Expected Salary: up to $40,000 a year

Wrap-Up

Since everyone loves pet treats, you can certainly make a profit. This can be a fun side business or a great full-time career depending on your business goals. Yet, you still have to treat this career as a business and do the necessary steps to be successful. The action steps in this chapter will help you.

Be sure to check with your town about regulations for having a business in your home and other possible business regulations.

If you are a creative person, you can design unique and fun treats that will delight the people that buy them and the animals who eat them. When you provide healthy and natural treats that are locally made and professionally marketed—your business will stand out.

14

ANIMAL ENERGY PRACTITIONER

Are you interested in the intuitive side of life and believe in the healing power of energy? Animal energy practitioners often use Reiki (Glossary) or other energy methods to help pets heal from all types of ailments. A certification in animal Reiki or some other form of energy healing is customary.

By becoming an animal energy practitioner, you can have a rewarding and lucrative career while helping pets restore themselves from emotional and physical ailments.

As an energy practitioner, you base your work with animals on the premise that all beings have energy flowing through them. When the energy is strong, the animal is healthy, balanced, and less likely to get ill. When the energy is weak, the animal is easily affected by stress and less resistant to illness. The job of an energy practitioner is to balance these energies to provide and maintain the pet's natural state.

This type of energy work is done hands-on or from a distance.

The practitioner uses his or her hands to channel the universal energy shared between the practitioner and client. Energy medicine (Glossary) is safe and works very well with conventional veterinary medicine, herbal medicine, homeopathy (Glossary), and Chinese medicine.

To become an energy practitioner, you should take a course in Reiki or some other form of energy healing before you begin promoting your business. Many practitioners like to use crystals (Glossary) and flower essences (Glossary) as part of their practice. These modalities provide more solutions for the pets you may encounter.

Once you complete a course and obtain certification, begin to practice on your pets, friends' companions, and local shelter animals to gain experience. Collect testimonials on your website.

You can then advertise online and distribute business cards promoting your healing business to local pet businesses. A woman I know who performs Reiki energy healing with animals advertises with a large magnetic sticker on her vehicle.

When you finish your training, you can open a practice where you utilize your compassion to help animals. As an animal energy practitioner, your work is to help them navigate through their life's challenges. With any professional practice, you will want to uphold your profession's code of ethics, which includes professional standard, confidentiality, education, etc.

You can work with a large number of animals, from horses to dogs to gerbils. Pet peeps want the best for their pets, and many of them are willing to try energy healing. You will find many grateful clients who are willing to pay up to $150 per hour for healing.

However, don't go into this for the money. Your heart must be in the right place to provide actual healing and comfort to animals.

Important Considerations

A large part of your job entails focus and personal awareness of your abilities. This means you may take on some of the energy of suffering pets. Learning to clear your energy and maintain inner peace is essential. The certification you choose will help you with this aspect of your practice.

Another part of your work may involve assisting the animal's person with their healing. People may be troubled or feel guilty over injuries or illnesses affecting their pets. Always be professional, compassionate, and practice good listening skills.

You must be ready for all types of situations as you progress with your career. You may encounter some very painful experiences—along with the wonderful and successful. Keep in mind that compassion fatigue is prevalent in this type of work.

Expected Salary: $60,000 a year

Wrap-Up

By becoming an animal Reiki or animal energy practitioner, you are joining a field that continues to grow in popularity. Holistic medicine and alternative therapies are now considered mainstream professions. Many animal people will seek this type of treatment for their companions.

Keep in mind it is important to invest in your future by getting the appropriate credentials, joining professional organizations, and building your practice with ethics and integrity. You want to provide your clients with the best possible care.

This profession takes stamina as well. You must believe that universal energy (Glossary) is shared by all beings. If you don't believe in holistic care and its effectiveness, you will not do well with this choice.

Do your research, speak to animal practitioners, and read blogs on the subject to decide if it is for you. Take a look at the action steps in this chapter as well.

If you are interested in running a kennel, read on. Chapter 15 covers the steps required to become a professional kennel owner.

Action Steps

1. Research online, speak to energy practitioners, read blogs, and take an introductory course to determine if this field is for you.
2. Download the free gift for helpful links on schools and organizations that support pet energy practitioners (https://wendyvandepoll.com/pet-jobs-free-gift).
3. Decide if you believe in the power of energetic healing and if you have the focus that it requires.
4. Learn Reiki through a course and gain a professional certification (Download Your Free Gift for the link).

5. Practice on shelter animals and your own animals to gain experience and reviews.
6. Advertise online and in person.
7. Take care of yourself by meditating, eating healthy, and spending time doing something you love to avoid compassion fatigue.

5. Practice on shelter animals and your own animals to gain experience and reviews.
6. Advertise online and in person.
7. Take care of yourself by meditating, eating healthy, and spending time doing something you love to avoid compassion fatigue.

Keep in mind it is important to invest in your future by getting the appropriate credentials, joining professional organizations, and building your practice with ethics and integrity. You want to provide your clients with the best possible care.

This profession takes stamina as well. You must believe that universal energy (Glossary) is shared by all beings. If you don't believe in holistic care and its effectiveness, you will not do well with this choice.

Do your research, speak to animal practitioners, and read blogs on the subject to decide if it is for you. Take a look at the action steps in this chapter as well.

If you are interested in running a kennel, read on. Chapter 15 covers the steps required to become a professional kennel owner.

Action Steps

1. Research online, speak to energy practitioners, read blogs, and take an introductory course to determine if this field is for you.
2. Download the free gift for helpful links on schools and organizations that support pet energy practitioners (https://wendyvandepoll.com/pet-jobs-free-gift).
3. Decide if you believe in the power of energetic healing and if you have the focus that it requires.
4. Learn Reiki through a course and gain a professional certification (Download Your Free Gift for the link).

15

KENNEL OWNER

Are you interested in boarding animals when their peeps go away? If so, you can start a kennel. You may need to rent or buy a space for a large kennel, or you can set up kennel facilities in your own home.

First, as with any business, do your research. Kennel operations require many moving parts. You must know about safety, health, behavior, and the ins and outs of the business. You will have to set up your kennel to accommodate the animals you choose to board. You will want to set up a yard, play areas, kennels, and feeding stations or food bowls.

You should also set up a station where you can bathe pets if necessary. Pet first aid kits and training are also essential. Be sure to obtain emergency vet information so that you can get help if something bad happens.

Second, set rates according to the services you offer. Market yourself online and leave flyers or business cards at local pet businesses. Attend business networking events and hand out your cards, since professionals are more likely to go out of town and require someone to board their pets.

Pet peeps will want to tour your facilities, so post pictures online and keep the facilities spotless and sterile. The better your facilities look—the more they will want to board with you. Whether you believe in vaccinations or not, it is probably a good idea to require animals to have full vaccinations.

You do want to prevent the spread of disease, as this could spoil your reputation fast. It is also best to require pets to be spayed or neutered—unless you are set up to accommodate animals in heat, etc.

When someone boards with you, be sure to learn the pet's schedule and adhere to it as much as possible. Pets are already stressed when they enter a new place; keeping their schedule can help calm them. Allow pets space to exercise and play by themselves throughout the day. Don't mix animals who don't know each other to prevent fighting.

Important Considerations

You must have a set-up that allows you to care for pets in the most efficient capacity. For dogs, you must have a yard and kennels set up. Also, you must be mindful of their feeding regimens.

Another consideration is keeping up with each boarder's medication schedule. Also be mindful that not all dogs get along. Get permission from the client if it is okay for their dog to play with others.

If you are doing this by yourself, you should limit the number of dogs you keep on hand (no more than three) to ensure that you deliver high-quality care to each one.

For cats, you must have a room where they can hide and feel safe. Understand that boarding is a very stressful situation for the pet, particularly cats, and you must set the pet at ease by providing the utmost safety. Studying an energy technique (Chapter 14) is a great service to add to calm your boarders.

Owners often worry about their pets while they are away. You can set their minds at ease by sending them daily updates. Be cordial and expect to be on call almost 24/7!

The initial start-up costs can be high. Don't cut corners to minimize costs. Pet people are always in need of safe, clean facilities to keep their pets in while they are gone on business or vacation. Run your business well and you will succeed.

Expected Salary: $58,165 per year

Wrap-Up

Running a kennel is hard but lucrative work. There are many moving parts, and it is essential you know what you are doing. Make sure you are up on town restrictions and other legalities before you open your business.

Since people are going to trust you with their animals, you must provide professional, ethical, and a stellar service for their companions. A dirty, poorly run, and neglectful kennel will quickly shut down.

There are many services you can add to your kennel operation.

You can offer massages (Chapter 16), grooming (Chapter 12), special walks, special diets, training, and more.

While start-up costs are high, you can expect to make an excellent salary with lots of hard work and attention to your clients. Your business will always be in demand!

Read on to the next chapter to learn how to become a pet massage therapist. Yes, pets can get massages, too! But don't forget your action steps.

Action Steps

1. Decide if running a kennel is for you. Do you like to be available to work 24/7 in the beginning? You must be willing to be available at all times just in case an emergency arises.
2. If this doesn't bother you—start your research. Look into facilities, town and state regulations, health regulations, etc.
3. You can download your free gift for associations and licensing information. (https://wendyvandepoll.com/pet-jobs-free-gift).
4. Once you are done with your research, set up your facilities with the appropriate needs for your boarders. Kennels, play areas, feeding stations, etc.
5. Start your marketing with a website, networking, open houses, etc.
6. Once you open your doors, make sure you keep your clients updated via video, texting, and/or emails.
7. Never falter from providing the best care for the

animals. Their people trust you, and your success will be riding on that trust.
8. Expect to dedicate your entire life to this venture until you can hire stellar employees.

16

PET MASSAGE THERAPIST

Do you love getting massages? My animal clients love to get their sore muscles worked on, and they need massages—just like we do. While some owners just want to spoil their pets with pampering that includes massages, others actually require massage for their pets to heal chronic pain and injuries.

You can work in equine massage, feline massage, canine massage, etc. You may work independently or with a company. Some places to look for work include animal shelters and rescues, racing barns, dressage barns, pet grooming salons, pet kennels, vet clinics, and independent breeders.

Massage therapy is a serious art which has medical uses. Therefore, you must attend school and become certified in order to learn appropriate techniques. Furthermore, some states restrict pet massage to veterinarians, while others allow vets to delegate work to trusted massage therapists.

There are still some states that don't regulate pet massage

therapy at all, but I still recommend certification. You want to be professional and a good business owner so potential clients trust the work you are doing is safe. Learn the laws in your state to see if this is a viable career in your area.

Look at different pet massage schools online and book appointments to visit the schools in person. You can expect to pay up to $8,000 for training. You may also consider completing a veterinary assistant program for a few thousand, as veterinary assistants are more likely to be paid well and be delegated work by veterinarians.

Build your reputation by working for a company or volunteering to massage in shelters. Using a website, you can market yourself with videos of your massages, testimonials from pet owners, and a display featuring your certification and training.

Be sure to take advantage of local businesses for referrals if you want to work independently. Your best bet to gain loyal clientele and steady work would be to work with a company or clinic.

Important Considerations

Pet massage can be a very physically demanding job. You must learn appropriate techniques to avoid injury to yourself and to your animal clients. You must also learn how to read a pet's body language to gauge how the animal is feeling.

With this career, you can be self-employed or work for a groomer, veterinarian, barn, etc.

Be prepared to get the proper training. Even if you are a licensed human massage therapist, you must learn the anatomy and physiology of the animals you are treating. Our four-legged friends do not have the same muscle structure as we do.

Expected Salary: $41,240 a year

Wrap-Up

Pet massage therapy is a great way to help horses, dogs, cats, and other animals recover from injuries or congenital defects. It is also a nice way to pamper pets! As long as you are ready for a physically exerting career, you will enjoy working in pet massage. Make sure pet massage is legal for non-vets in your state before you proceed.

Pet massage certification couples nicely with energy work, veterinarian medicine, day care, pet sitting, and more as an add-on to the services you may offer.

Before you learn how to start a doggie day care—where dogs can have fun and play outside of their homes—check out the action steps for this chapter!

A doggie day care is a great way to earn some cash while enjoying time spent with four-legged friends. I can't think of a career that is more fun.

Action Steps

1. Determine if you have the physical strength to give massages to animals.
2. If you do, then research laws in your state to make sure you can practice animal massage. The last thing

you want to have happen is to spend a bunch of money and time to get certified and find out later you can't practice.
3. If it is legal for a non-veterinarian to carry out animal massage, get certified. Find a school where you actually have hands-on experience with animals.
4. Schools and licensing/certification/professional organizations are listed in your free gift (https://wendyvandepoll.com/pet-jobs-free-gift).
5. After certification, seek a job at local pet businesses and vet clinics to build your business.
6. Build your reputation and testimonials through volunteer work.
7. And of course, create your website and be involved on social media to build your following and client base.

17

DOGGIE DAY CARE OWNER

Would you love to operate a business where doggos get to visit you every day? Pet day care centers are places where owners can drop off their dogs for a few hours each day. People may do this to socialize their pets or to ensure their pets are cared for while they are at work.

You typically charge by the hour and spend those hours playing with and socializing pets. You can even offer massages (Chapter 16) as an additional service. It is important to know how many dogs you can handle. You must set a limit on how many pets you can care for because you want to provide quality time for each animal.

You can open a facility or run your doggie day care from your home. You must have a large space where dogs can play, as well as lots of available toys. In addition, you may need kennels so pups can have a quiet, safe space to rest.

You also should consider your energy level. It takes a lot of energy to keep up with the needs of the animals! And remember to research prices of other local pet day cares and set your own based on the industry average.

Also, set your hours based on when people are most likely to be at work, as this is when pet owners will need you the most.

While you don't need any education to become a dog day care owner, you can benefit from certifications in emergency pet care, animal behavior, or even veterinary assistance. These skills make you more marketable and give owners peace of mind.

You can give owners even more peace of mind by learning what care pet peeps expect from you. Offer to feed the food and treats their companions are used to. Finally, check with your local town ordinances to find out what sorts of permits and licenses you need for this kind of business.

Advertise at local pet stores and kennels. Mention all of the services you offer. Invite people to tour your day care and contact you for free price quotes.

When a new dog joins your day care, introduce it gradually to the other dogs to prevent fighting and injuries. If pets do get into a fight, swiftly separate them and put them in their respective kennels to "cool off."

Alternatively, if you don't want to open a dog day care of your own or you want to try the business before opening your own, you can apply to work at a local dog day care. You may earn minimum wage, but you will have a fun job with animals that you will love!

Important Considerations

A doggie day care puts you in charge of the health and happiness of many pets for several hours a day. You must dedicate your full energy to the job and supervise the pets in your care. You must have the energy to play with them and keep them occupied.

A dog day care is a great way to make some cash. But you can also offer other services, such as grooming or massage, alongside the basic pet care service you are offering. Expand your services slowly as you build a clientele, gain reviews, and learn what people in your area want. Doing too much at once can raise your start-up costs and overwhelm you.

Expected Salary: $30,000 a year or more

Wrap-Up

If you want to provide pet peeps a valuable service and take care of dogs all day—running a pet day care can be a great career for you. Alternatively, you can apply to work at a local dog day care. It is a fun career, but it requires a lot of energy and responsibility.

There is a lot of responsibility that goes into a doggie day care because you are taking care of someone's beloved companion. Be sure your facility is clean and you have the proper trainings to gain professionalism in your industry.

In Chapter 18, I talk about becoming a veterinarian. This is an amazing profession and has many specialties to choose from. Although it is a financial and educational commitment, becoming a veterinarian is a worthy aspiration. Read on to learn how to become one! But don't forget your action steps.

Action Steps

1. Volunteer or work at a doggie day care center to determine if this is the type of work you want to do.
2. If so, learn about local ordinances and licenses for your type of business. You want to do this before you invest in your business.
3. Obtain certification in animal-related disciplines if desired. This is a good idea to show your people clients you are professional and their animals are safe.
4. Decide where you want to set up your facilities. Home or a separate building.
5. Research fees of your competition and then fair prices based on local pricing trends.
6. Advertise your business using a website, social media, local newspaper, etc.
7. Play with pets and care for their needs. Supervise them well.
8. Offer additional services if desired.

18

VETERINARIAN

Have you always dreamed about become a veterinarian? I know I did when I was a kid. Becoming a veterinarian is a dream for many people. While it requires a great deal of education, it can be a lucrative and rewarding career, a career where you get to work with animals and save lives every day.

To start, you must obtain a bachelor's degree in a field such as biology, zoology, chemistry, microbiology, physiology, or animal husbandry. You must earn high grades while in high school and college. Getting into a veterinarian school tends to be a very competitive process.

After you acquire your undergraduate degree, apply to a school of veterinary medicine to complete a doctorate of veterinary medicine (DVM), which can take up to four years. Veterinarian school consists of all-day classes and rigorous testing in subjects like pathophysiology and anatomy. You will have lots of studying and memorizing to do when you're not in class.

To augment your education, you should join a pre-vet club at your school and volunteer at vet clinics or animal shelters. Some veterinarians also start by working as veterinarian techs. You can expect to pay about $250,000 for your doctorate.

Once you finish school, you have to become licensed by taking the state board exam for veterinary medicine. While this exam is tough, school will prepare you for it. After you pass the exam, you can apply to work at veterinarian clinics to gain experience. Typically, you should have years of experience before starting your own clinic.

Important Considerations

Working as a veterinarian is a lucrative and rewarding career. However, there are some things you need to consider first. Veterinarians need to be emotionally strong because of the wide variety of issues they may encounter in the field.

You may see some horrible things, such as chronically ill, abused, or critically injured pets. Part of your job will involve euthanizing, which can be emotionally wrenching for both the staff and pet families. While these parts of the job can be emotionally hard, they are still very important.

Veterinarians may encounter pets who are scared to be in the office. They may try to bite or scratch. Fortunately, you will learn many ways to prevent this in school as well as through experience. I also touch on how to handle difficult pets in Chapter 32.

You can make significant money as a veterinarian. However, if you are in it just for money, you are in it for the wrong reasons. A love of pets and a desire to make a positive difference in the world should be your motivation to enter this career. Since becoming a veterinarian takes a lot of schooling, you must be motivated and truly interested in the career.

It can be hard to afford school, especially since you will not have time to work throughout your training. Therefore, it may be helpful to save money, apply for grants and scholarships, take out student loans, and even enter the military for help with education costs.

Working as a veterinarian entails standing on your feet for long hours, being on call most hours of the day, and having few vacation days. You may work weekends and holidays.

Expected Salary: starting at $60,000 a year, up to $170,000 with experience

Wrap-Up

Becoming a veterinarian is a rigorous and competitive process. Working as a veterinarian entails being on call and witnessing some emotionally challenging things. You must be ready to manage your fatigue and burnout, as it is a demanding profession.

Even though school is expensive and a long process, this career can be satisfying, as you can make a huge difference in the lives of pets and their people.

After reading this chapter, do the action steps. If you decide you don't want to become a veterinarian but you want to work in animal medicine, consider becoming a veterinarian technician. The next chapter teaches you everything about how to become one!

Action Steps

1. Ask a local veterinarian office if you can observe the practice for a day or couple of hours. This will give you an idea of the events that happen in a practice. Be honest with yourself and ask, "Is this for me?"
2. Complete a bachelor's in a science field, as I explained in this chapter. Strive for excellent grades, as the competition is tough to get into veterinarian school.
3. Join a pre-vet club, volunteer with animals, or work as a veterinarian technician or assistant.
4. Apply to veterinarian school and earn a DVM. Be involved with as much as you can so you get high grades and excellent experience.
5. Get licensed through your state board.
6. Work for a clinic for a while before you open your practice to gain business experience as well as practical experience.
7. Open your own practice if desired.
8. Download your free gift with helpful links (https://wendyvandepoll.com/pet-jobs-free-gift).

19

VETERINARY TECHNICIAN

Would you like to assist a veterinarian with various tasks? Veterinary technicians are to veterinarians what nurses are to doctors. You will perform a wide variety of tasks, from sanitizing equipment to providing anesthesia to clipping pets' toenails.

You are often the first person pets and their owners encounter in the veterinarian office, and you will interview owners to gather crucial information for the vet. Your place of employment will be in a veterinarian clinic, humane society, or with a mobile veterinarian.

Becoming a veterinary technician entails an associate's degree in veterinary technology, which equates to about two years of schooling. Some schools are online, such as Penn Foster and San Juan College.

Others are hands-on programs, which give you more practical skills. Even online programs require you to spend a few weeks in practical hands-on training as an intern at a veterinarian clinic. Make sure your state allows for online schooling.

Once you complete your schooling, you must become licensed with your state board by taking a veterinary technology exam. Upon passing the exam, you can apply for jobs with veterinarian clinics or other facilities. Depending on your state, you may have to take continuing education classes to keep your license current.

Important Considerations

Working as a veterinary technician allows you to work directly with animals and provide life-saving support. It puts you in the forefront of veterinary medicine. You will be on your feet for long hours, and you may encounter challenging people and their animals.

While your school will train you how to handle all of these issues, you must be prepared for them as you choose to enter this career. These problems are typically far and few between; most veterinary technicians say that they love working with animals and couldn't ask for a better job!

Veterinary technicians also must practice great customer service, as they are often the face of the clinics. You must calm and comfort anxious or grieving pet owners, soothe scared pets, and address all issues for the veterinarian.

Expected Salary: $25,000–$35,000 a year

Wrap-Up

This career lets you handle animals and save lives! Becoming a veterinary technician involves some of the same aspects of working as a veterinarian for a fraction of the schooling and cost. However, it also pays significantly less.

You will be responsible for keeping the schedule moving so that the veterinarian doesn't run late, assisting the veterinarian with exams, cleaning treatment rooms, initial patient contact, and many other duties.

As you work through the action steps, do your research by asking other veterinary technicians what they love and what they find challenging in their jobs.

Would you like to work hands-on with horses specifically? In Chapter 20, you will learn about how to become a barn manager.

Action Steps

1. Interview veterinary technicians about the pros and cons of their career.
2. Decide if you want to obtain an online degree, blended degree (Glossary), or face-to-face training.
3. Apply to and complete a veterinary technician degree.
4. Get your license and search for a position in a facility that meets your career goals.
5. Research educational opportunities as a licensed

veterinary technician to stay current with industry standards.
6. Download your free gift that has helpful resources to get you started (https://wendyvandepoll.com/pet-jobs-free-gift).

20

BARN MANAGER

Do you want to combine your love for horses with business? As a barn manager, you are the one in charge of feeding and grooming, exercise schedules, turnout schedules, transportation, showing schedules, brand inspections, and veterinarian and farrier appointments.

You must order necessary supplies, direct employees, handle payroll, and fix emergency situations. You also must ensure the barn is kept clean, manage the prevention of diseases, and have strict precautions against injuries.

The smooth operation of a horse barn is your job! You will be in charge of horses and people alike.

There are different kinds of barns that you can work in. Some are for horses that race or show in dressage, etc. Others are for boarding horses for people that cannot have a horse on their own property. There are also barns in need of a manager where they rescue unwanted animals. Your tasks will be influenced by the type of barn you work in.

The main component of being a barn manager is developing extensive equine knowledge and experience. If you grew up around horses, you have a head start, but you can also gain experience by working in a horse barn. Taking courses in equine medicine, massage (Chapter 16), energy healing (Chapter 14), and pet care can also help you get the expertise you need.

Learn about payroll and other skills useful for a barn. You can find cheap or free classes online for these things. Furthermore, you should possess basic computer and filing skills. Most community colleges offer classes on computer skills and business administration for low prices.

When you find an opening for a position as a barn manager, you want to prove that you have what it takes. Be prepared to show off your office skills and your equine knowledge. You will probably be asked to handle a horse as well.

If you want to open your own barn, you must invest money in purchasing or building a facility and obtaining all the necessary supplies, equipment, horses, and employees. Create a business plan and formulate a solid idea of how you will manage your barn.

Barn management can be an extremely lucrative career, and there are colleges now that offer associate's and bachelor's degrees in equine studies.

Important Considerations

Barn managers have very important jobs, and they have a lot of responsibility. Expect long hours and lots of work. Also, expect to be on call even at night and on holidays should anything go wrong in the barn.

To excel at this career, you must love working with horses and people. You must not be above office work or outside work that gets you dirty. You will have to be flexible and take on a wide variety of tasks and duties.

The entire barn operation relies on you, so you will have pressure to perform exceptionally well. You will also have immense control over the barn and the ability to make decisions.

Expected Salary: $67,950

Wrap-Up

Barn managers do so many things and become the entire foundation of a successful barn operation. As a barn manager, you will work with people and horses every day. This career can be stressful, but fun and rewarding as well. If you love horses, this is an excellent career to get started in.

Before you jump into becoming a barn manager, go over the action steps in this chapter. They will help you streamline the process.

To augment the work of veterinarians, you can become a veterinary acupuncturist or chiropractor. The next two chapters detail how you can enter these rewarding careers in animal medicine and care.

Action Steps

1. Research colleges to obtain an associate's or bachelor's degree in equine studies.
2. Become skilled in working with and around horses if you don't have the experience.
3. Decide if you can manage many tasks at one time. Being a barn manager requires organization, knowledge, and careful planning.
4. Work at an established barn for a while to gain experience before you invest in schooling.
5. Graduate from the college of your choice. Then consider opening your own barn. Obtain a space and acquire appropriate licenses. Create a business plan for success. Then stock and staff the barn.

21

VETERINARY ACUPUNCTURIST

Are you holistically minded, and do you want to be a veterinarian? Then consider acupuncture once you become a DVM. Although in some states it is legal to become an acupuncturist without a DVM, do your research before you start your training.

Acupuncture is the ancient Chinese art of using needles to relieve pressure at certain points throughout the body to treat maladies. In recent years, Western medicine has realized the high success rates of acupuncture, and the military even offers acupuncture to their members now. Animal medicine is no different. You can find a lucrative career in the animal medicine industry with veterinary acupuncture.

Veterinary acupuncture treats many things:

- Injuries
- Chronic pain
- Digestive issues

- Infertility
- Anxiety
- And more

If a pet has an issue, stimulating certain points on his or her body can bring about the results a pet's person desires. This service oftentimes offers a solution or critical piece of the pet healthcare puzzle.

To offer this service, you must attend an acupuncture training program. You can find a program on the website for the American Board of Animal Acupuncture or a Google search. This program will probably take about two years, depending on your rate of completion.

The American Board of Animal Acupuncture offers certification. This certification is legally required in most states (as is veterinarian licensure). The test is mostly written. After getting certified, you will have to attend continuing education every year through the American Board of Animal Acupuncture to keep your certification current.

You can add acupuncture to your current practice or travel to barns, breeding facilities, farms, other veterinary clinics, show rings, racetracks, kennels, zoos, etc. This career can be exciting and lucrative if you love helping animals and feel a pull toward Chinese and alternative medicine.

Important Considerations

Acupuncture is an amazing way to help facilitate health and healing in pets. Do your research to be sure you can be a practicing veterinary acupuncturist without being a licensed DVM.

Honestly, I wouldn't recommend this field without becoming a veterinarian first. In most states and countries, acupuncture is considered to be a surgical procedure.

Animals have many differences in anatomy. There is also a potential to do harm if your treatments are done incorrectly. A DVM has extensive training with disease, anatomy and physiology, structural issues, etc. Without this degree, you risk not being able to treat an animal correctly. That said, if it is legal in your state, you can work under a veterinarian with the proper certification.

Expected Salary: $49,000 a year, considerably more if you are a DVM

Wrap-Up

Acupuncture is becoming more and more accepted in Western medicine as a viable means of promoting and maintaining healing and health. You can practice it on animals with stunning results. Work alongside veterinarians or independently to help animals.

The more you know about traditional Chinese medicine and philosophies and the Western scientific background, the more you can treat the animals under your care properly.

In the next chapter, you will learn more about becoming a veterinary chiropractor. But first, take a look at the action steps in this chapter to determine if acupuncture is for you.

While becoming an animal chiropractor is perhaps even more

challenging than becoming a veterinarian, animal chiropractors have rewarding jobs with high pay.

Action Steps

1. Ask a local veterinary acupuncturist or human acupuncturist if you can observe the practice for a day or a couple of hours. This will give you an idea if you are ready to commit to hard work.
2. Research your state's laws about practicing without a veterinarian license. Obviously, if it is not legal, you don't want to spent the time and money to get a degree you can't use.
3. Apply to veterinarian school and earn a DVM if acupuncture without a license is not legal.
4. Get licensed through your state board and continue your education.
5. Work for a clinic for a while before you open your practice to gain business experience as well as practical experience.
6. Open your own practice if desired.
7. Download your free gift for veterinary acupuncture organizations (https://wendyvandepoll.com/pet-jobs-free-gift).

22

VETERINARIAN CHIROPRACTOR

Have you ever thought it was possible that animals could benefit from chiropractic care? Just like humans who need their necks adjusted or their backs manipulated into place, so do animals.

Dogs, cats, horses, and all other types of vertebrates sometimes need alignments. Pets in special need of chiropractic services include animals…

- Who have been injured.
- With congenital deformities.
- Who work hard, such as racehorses, police dogs, or service animals.

As an animal chiropractor, you will work closely with veterinarians to provide much-needed skeletal alignment services to animals.

Most veterinarian chiropractors are DVMs, or doctors of

veterinary medicine, themselves. If you become a veterinarian (Chapter 18), you may choose to specialize in chiropractic medicine. If you choose this specialty, you will attend additional clinics and training in chiropractic skills, usually for seventy-five to one hundred hours.

The American Veterinary Medical Association lists various schools that offer this training on their website (Resources). These are postgraduate programs for licensed veterinarians; you must have a license to register for them. The costs vary for these programs.

When you complete your hours in the course, you will sit for the Animal Chiropractic Certification Commission Exam, which contains practical and written portions to ensure you have the necessary knowledge to practice. You cannot work in this field without this certification.

With the certification in hand, you can work in a variety of settings. You can start a traveling practice that visits animal in their homes or other settings. It will be important to promote yourself online and at animal-related events. You can also work for a barn or numerous veterinarian clinics as a traveling chiropractor.

Once you graduate and are certified, you must complete up to thirty hours of continuing education training each year to keep your certification current. You will learn new skills and advancements in animal medicine.

Important Considerations

Animal chiropractors go through extensive education, but that education is certainly worthwhile. You will earn an excellent salary, provide helpful pain relief to animals, and facilitate healing in sick and injured animals. You have a lot of choices when it comes to where you work.

This job is very physical and requires long hours on your feet. You must have the strength to perform the duties, which can become more strenuous depending on the type of animal you choose to work with. For instance, equine chiropractors must have intense upper body strength; a dog chiropractor may not need as much upper body strength. You will often work on weekends and even holidays, and you may be on call.

Expected Salary: $62,424 a year

Wrap-Up

Working as a veterinary chiropractor allows you to treat joint conditions and injuries in animals. You can work in a huge variety of settings on all types of animals. Your job is highly specialized, and, if you develop your business properly, your services can be of high demand.

Once you graduate and are licensed as a veterinarian, there are various programs for animal chiropractic medicine you can apply to. This is a rewarding career that can offer many possibilities for growth and continued education.

So far, you have explored many options for careers and businesses in the pet industry. We talked about working with animals, both in person and online. Now let's get into how to volunteer with animals.

Volunteering means you work with animals for little or no pay, but it can add significant meaning and contentment to your life. Get involved in your animal community today by starting the next section of this book.

But first, to get a quick overview as to what is involved with becoming a successful animal chiropractor, go to the action steps for this chapter.

Action Steps

1. Determine where you want to go to veterinarian school. After you have your DVM, research animal chiropractic certification trainings.
2. Download your free gift for veterinary chiropractic organizations (https://wendyvandepoll.com/pet-jobs-free-gift).
3. Chiropractor certification programs are approximately seventy-five to one hundred hours in length. Decide on the program you want to attend.
4. After you receive your certification, determine if you want to be a traveling chiropractor or work in your office. Also decide which type of animal you want to work with.
5. Be sure to keep up with your required thirty hours of continuing education a year.

SECTION III

VOLUNTEER

Is it your goal to do good for the animals of the world regardless if you are paid or not?

Volunteering would be the perfect choice. In this section, I will cover a variety of volunteer positions you can explore. Some of the career choices I cover can actually be paid positions as well. I included them in this section because I wanted to give you the chance to choose the right one according to your goals.

Volunteering is Wonderful

1. You get the needed experience as you prepare for other careers mentioned in this book.
2. You can do what you love in your spare time.

3. You will make a tremendous difference for many animals and pet families.

23

HUMANE SOCIETY/RESCUE VOLUNTEER

Do you want to save pets from abandonment, abuse, or neglect? If you answered yes, you can become a rescue worker. Rescue workers save the lives of animals and keep them out of kill shelters—where they are euthanized if they are not adopted quickly enough.

Often, this job does not pay anything, but you can obtain many government grants and individual donations to cover expenses. You can also rely on volunteers for labor.

You may volunteer at a rescue or open one of your own. To start volunteering, visit local rescues and ask if they need help. Your hours will be flexible, so you can put in as much time as you want. Your duties will involve:

- Walking
- Bathing
- Cleaning up after animals
- Going along on rescues

- Attending community outreach events, like adoption events
- Feeding
- Socializing

To open your own rescue, it is best to have a large facility with lots of room for animals to be safe and comfortable. You may be able to get a federal or state grant for all your equipment and start-up costs.

Before you apply for grants, come up with a mission statement that summarizes your interest in helping animals and the needs you plan to serve in your community. You will also need to draft a business plan to show where any money you receive will go.

There are different types of shelters. For a no-kill shelter, you accept potentially adoptable pets and never euthanize them, except for incurable illness or injury. Sanctuaries are lifelong habitats for animals where they are never euthanized unless necessary. All of these rescues entail caring for animals and attempting to get them adopted. Decide which one you want to operate.

It is best to forge partnerships with local veterinarians, pet food suppliers, and other local shelters so that you can get supplies and resources at a low cost. Be sure to post ads soliciting the community for donations to help animals in need.

You want to assemble a team of volunteer and/or paid workers, depending on your budget. Seek out people who are true animal lovers and who have prior shelter or rescue experience.

You can take on rescue pets from high-kill and/or no-kill shelters. You can also acquire them through other rescue organizations. Contact local rescue organizations and the ASPCA to find out how to get started. You may also contact Animal Control and let them know that you will take on some of the animals that they rescue. Getting involved in the community is probably the most crucial part of becoming a rescue founder.

Your opening day should be a big event with lots of press and advertising. Host monthly adoption events to further spread awareness about your organization, recruit volunteers, and get animals adopted out. You can also put up flyers and cards to raise awareness. Many rescues also participate in spay and neuter clinics. These clinics prevent overpopulation of pets.

Important Considerations

As a rescue worker, you will work long hours for little or no money. You will encounter many difficult situations, including severely sick and abused animals. This can be emotionally difficult, so make sure you are prepared for compassion fatigue, which could lead to burnout. I cover this in my book, *The Pet Professional's Guide to Pet Loss Grief: How to Prevent Burnout, Support Clients, and Manage the Business of Grief.*

Despite the difficulties and hardship that go along with this position, always remember you are saving many lives and serving one of your community's biggest needs.

Wrap-Up

The life of a rescue worker can be exhausting and thankless. But when you look into the eyes of every animal you rescue, you will realize why you are doing this.

Getting started can be challenging, but once you become a part of your local rescue community, you will enjoy much success.

To learn how to help people in need and work with animals, read the next chapter about becoming a service animal trainer, but first, check out your action steps.

Action Steps

1. Download your free gift for a list of humane society, rescue associations and rescue organizations (https://wendyvandepoll.com/pet-jobs-free-gift).
2. Volunteer at a local rescue to determine if you want to do this type of work.
3. Get a business plan and mission statement together if you decide you have the stamina to witness neglect, abuse, and other unpleasant events regarding animals.
4. Obtain the funding you need to open your rescue.
5. Set up your facilities so the animals are safe and comfortable.
6. Get a good team together. It can be difficult to do this work by yourself. When you have a great team with designated jobs, the process can go much smoother.
7. Spread the word through lots of events and

advertising. Participate in community education about responsible spaying and neutering.

24

SERVICE ANIMAL TRAINER

Have you seen the service animals in their black or bright orange uniforms guiding people through their daily activities and reacted with a smile? These animals offer companionship and help to their person. The following are a few types of service animals. This is not a full list. You can do a Google search to find out more.

Here are some examples of service dogs:

- Seeing eye dogs for people with vision impairment
- Scent dogs who can alert their owners to oncoming diabetic or epileptic crises
- Guide dogs for the hearing impaired or wheelchair bound

These dogs work hard and faithfully to help their companions through everyday life. Companions and service animals often

24

SERVICE ANIMAL TRAINER

Have you seen the service animals in their black or bright orange uniforms guiding people through their daily activities and reacted with a smile? These animals offer companionship and help to their person. The following are a few types of service animals. This is not a full list. You can do a Google search to find out more.

Here are some examples of service dogs:

- Seeing eye dogs for people with vision impairment
- Scent dogs who can alert their owners to oncoming diabetic or epileptic crises
- Guide dogs for the hearing impaired or wheelchair bound

These dogs work hard and faithfully to help their companions through everyday life. Companions and service animals often

advertising. Participate in community education about responsible spaying and neutering.

become extremely close and attached to one another, forming an unbreakable partnership.

Service animal trainers typically work on a volunteer basis for organizations or individually, though some are paid. To get started, you should start by gaining experience working with dogs. You may become a certified dog trainer or simply have dogs of your own. Volunteering at a dog shelter is another way to get comfortable with dogs and make a great, memorable difference in the world.

Once you have some dog experience, you must enroll in a program. There are many programs out there that teach basic techniques. While these programs can get you familiar with the training methods used, they are not sufficient to become a certified service animal trainer.

Reputable programs offered through universities or specific dog training schools take two to three years and require a three-year apprenticeship. Costs will vary but can reach the tens of thousands. The free gift that goes with this book has the two associations that recommend legitimate trainings (Resources).

Before you enter school, it is best to contact other service animal trainers and gain an apprenticeship. Getting into service training schools is a competitive process, so having an apprenticeship and some experience will give you a leg up. Work hard alongside your mentor and pay attention. You won't be paid, but the education and hands-on practice you get will be priceless.

After three hundred hours of training, completion of a course, and three references in the training field, you can sit for an exam with the Certification Council for Professional Dog Trainers (Resources). If you pass, you will have a certificate. This certificate is not mandatory by law, but most organizations won't hire you unless you possess it. A few states do require a special license as well, which your school will inform you about and prepare you for.

Begin volunteering with an organization or offering training on an individual basis. You may also want to volunteer in a prison dog program and teach prisoners how to train service animals, which I cover in more detail in Chapter 25. As you gain experience, you can post testimonials, videos of you training, and videos of your trained dogs working as service animals as a sort of portfolio on your website.

The best places to advertise include rescue organizations, agility organizations, pet stores, doctors' offices, and disability offices. You should also consider reaching out to places like schools for the visually impaired or schools for the hearing impaired. By networking with other animal professionals, you can make your business known so that they can refer people who need service animal training to you.

Definitely consider working with shelter dogs. If you can train viable shelter dogs to become service animals, they instantly become much more adoptable. You give them a new lease on life and help out people with disabilities who need a canine companion.

Consider offering service animal training alongside other forms of dog training, such as obedience or agility training. You can make more money and attract more clients if you expand your training services.

Important Considerations

Service animal training requires education and time. While it does not pay well, if at all, it is a highly lucrative career in terms of making a difference in the world.

You will have the opportunity to work with animals and help people with challenges as you show them how to work with their new service animal.

This is a job you will need to train for. There is a lot that goes into the position—education, experience, patience, and compassion are necessary.

Expected Salary: $34,000 a year or volunteer basis

Wrap-Up

Service animal training is a lovely way to make a difference in the lives of both animals and humans. After completing your education, you can work in a variety of settings and help many individuals gain security and independence with the help of animals.

Your skills will always be in high demand, so you will likely find business anywhere you live. To make extra money, you can offer service animal training along with other forms of dog training.

I mentioned prison dog programs earlier. Now, you might be wondering how to get involved. You may be wondering what prison dog programs are. In the next chapter, I will show you how to get involved in these super helpful rehabilitative programs!

Here are your action steps for this chapter. Training dogs for service is a great choice if you want to help people become more independent and train dogs to assist.

Action Steps

1. Gain experience with training dogs first and become a certified dog trainer (Chapter 11). This will give you training skills as well as an additional career to add to your service dog training ventures.
2. Attend an educational program for service dog training. Download your free gift for the associations that list legitimate trainings (Resources).
3. Sit for certification and any legally required licensing in your state.
4. Work with an organization, such as a shelter or prison dog program.
5. Market yourself in places where people who are looking for service animal training are likely to go.
6. Combine service animal training with other training services to secure a viable income.

25

PRISON DOG TRAINER/HANDLER

Would you like to be involved with a community service program that helps prisoners and shelter dogs? This is a wonderful community outreach program. Statistics show that hundreds of dogs that were taken out of shelters and then handled and trained by prisoners became more adoptable.

This program not only saves animals, but it enriches the lives of prisoners and helps with their rehabilitation. These programs have had such a positive impact on communities. A study shows that prisoners are much less likely to return to prison if they worked in a dog training program.

Some prisons work exclusively with dogs, but some, like Ohio Reformatory for Women, also involve wildlife rehabilitation and other types of animals. The prisoners will keep the animals in their cells and provide for their care around the clock. They will socialize, groom, and care for them. In addition, the prisoners are also involved in training.

Prisoners often have more time on their hands than other people, making them excellent volunteers. They have more proven success than other types of volunteers in training service dogs for this very reason. You can help rehabilitate prisoners, train service animals, and make shelter dogs more adoptable by volunteering in one of these programs.

To get involved in this program, look up "local prison dog programs." If there is one in your area, you can contact them to find out how to get involved. You will need to pass a background check and prove that you have experience in dog training.

Important Considerations

Prisoners are screened before becoming dog handlers and earn the privilege of working with dogs. Don't worry—animal abusers are not going to be in the program! Most of the people in the program may have criminal history, but they love animals and genuinely want to do their part to help the world.

You can meet many wonderful people and make a huge difference by volunteering with them. Often, the only thing these prisoners have to look forward to is their time with their dogs.

You won't make any money doing this, but the rewards are so much greater than the money! Many prisoners in the program have helped produce over four hundred adoptable dogs or service animals. In addition, many of these animals were on death row in shelters and now have a new lease on life.

Wrap-Up

Prison dog programs are effective programs changing the lives of animals and prisoners for the better. Animals with nowhere to go and criminals with no hope are able to find love and happiness with each other. The program benefits prisoners, who often learn important life skills and don't return to prison later on after release.

You and the prisoner assigned to you will share custody of the dog while in training. It is important for the dog to have experience with living in someone's home prior to adoption.

There aren't many action steps for this volunteer position, but they will help you stay focused if you want to get involved with this great community project.

Now, if you are interested in opening your home to pets waiting to be adopted, then read on to learn how to become a pet foster parent. This volunteer opportunity requires a big heart, an open home, and some pet food!

Action Steps

1. Learn about local prison dog programs. Search Google as a start to see if there are any in your area.
2. Download your free gift for suggested programs (https://wendyvandepoll.com/pet-jobs-free-gift).
3. Sign up to volunteer. If they don't have any open positions for working with prisoners, consider volunteering in the office, etc. This will get you known within the organization.

4. Keep in mind you are providing an excellent service. You are helping to save the lives of unwanted dogs as well as giving an inmate the opportunity to be successful.

26

FOSTER PARENT

Would you love to open your home to animals who are in need of a temporary home before they get adopted? Becoming a foster parent has many benefits. You can choose:

- How many animals you will foster
- When you want to foster
- What type of animal you would like to help

I never fostered an animal, but all my rescue dogs who lived in a foster home prior to adoption have been wonderful. They have been socialized and some even trained.

My friend, Robin, fostered a dog that I will never forget. This little guy was a poodle cross. Freddy had been found wandering the street—abandoned. No one knew his history. Robin took him into her home, groomed his scraggly tangled hair, and fed him.

Freddy looked at Robin with so much adoration in his eyes—I

could tell he was truly grateful. After a few weeks, a rescue group for poodles was ready for Freddy, and he left. Robin and I cried, but we both were happy. I received an update one week later—Freddy had been adopted by a lovely couple! The rescue sent Robin a picture of them holding him. We didn't even recognize him with his new haircut.

Fostering gives a pet who is up for adoption a temporary place to stay out of the shelter. You are not only freeing up space in shelters, but you are also socializing and handling these animals to make them more adoptable. You may keep a pet for a few days to a few months, but your role in his or her life is very important.

Some organizations may let you adopt the pets you foster and grow attached to. Others won't. However, you still get to spend time working hands-on with a pet and getting him or her ready for a forever home.

Contact your local rescues and shelters to learn about local foster programs. They will tell you who to contact to get started. You will probably have to fill out an application and possibly even pass a background check, which is more concerned with crimes against animals or abuse than anything else.

The person in charge of the program will probably visit your home to ensure that you will be able to care for the pet. Once you are approved, you may get a new foster pet the same day, or you may have to wait a while before a pet is ready to enter your home.

If your community doesn't have a foster program, you can start one by volunteering to take in animals at local crowded humane society shelters. By volunteering at a humane society shelter, you can also learn a lot about rescue work and perform many of the same functions as a foster parent. The shelter may let you take animals home, especially if it is near capacity.

Important Considerations

You may fall in love with your new friend, and then you will have to send him or her on to his or her new home. This could be difficult. Always remember you touched his or her life in a way he or she will never forget. You helped this animal get one step closer to a sanctuary or forever home.

Let this thought help you through the sense of loss you may feel. In time, you will get used to seeing pets come and go from your home, so you will be able to avoid becoming attached to every cute dog or cat you take in.

Some pets will be absolutely wonderful. Others will be more difficult. Part of your job as a foster pet parent is socializing the animal and getting him or her used to humans so that he or she becomes more adoptable.

Furthermore, you have to get the foster pet used to your pets through gradual introduction and supervised play time. Socializing the foster pet with your pets will be another important step in getting him or her ready for a forever home.

You will be responsible for a pet's veterinary care, grooming, food, and other supplies while he or she is in your care. While some organizations will help offset these costs, some won't be able to. The cost of fostering a pet is small compared to the rewards you gain, however.

Wrap-Up

If you are not ready to adopt a pet, but you want to make a difference in the animal community of your area, then please consider becoming a foster pet parent. While the work is not always easy, it is certainly impactful for you and for the pet. Your lives will be forever changed for the better, and you will have beautiful memories of so many animals you have helped.

You have the choice of when you want to take animals in, the type of animal you are willing to share your home with, and the number. In fact, if you want to take a break from this position, you can just alert the organization you volunteer for that you will be taking a vacation, need to be out of town, or you just need your home to care for your own animals.

The action steps in this chapter will provide you with the top tasks you need to carry out in order to get started.

Working with wildlife is an interesting and challenging form of volunteer work that you can get involved in. The next chapter will show you how!

Action Steps

1. Sign up for a local foster organization. Contact shelters, search for rescue groups, and ask breeders for leads on how to become a foster parent.
2. Pass a background check and home inspection. This is necessary for the animal's safety. The last thing that needs to happen is for an animal to be placed in a foster home of an abuser.

3. Love the pets you foster, socialize them, and handle them in various situations and environments.
4. Be ready to pay for their care as a foster parent. Always ask the agency you volunteer for if any fees are covered.
5. When the pet is ready to go to a sanctuary or get adopted, you may be responsible to transport it or bring it to a place for transport.
6. If there is no foster program in your area, you can start one by volunteering to foster at your local humane society.

27

WILDLIFE REHABILITATOR

Do you love nature and wild animals? If you do, you will thrive as a wildlife rehabilitator. Wildlife rehabilitators are the responders who help clean up animals impacted by oil spills. This can be a paid as well as a volunteer position.

A wildlife rehabilitator rescues and rehabilitates injured wildlife and then releases them back into the wild. They also play an integral role in educating the public about wildlife to prevent some of the mistakes people make. Plus, they spend many hours raising money to support their mission.

Most rehabilitators have degrees in biology or zoology, but you don't have to have a degree to enter the field. It is best to contact your local U.S. Fish and Wildlife Service and local state Fish and Game to learn about permits in your area before you even get started, as a permit may be required to even volunteer with an established wildlife agency or individual organization.

Working with an established wildlife rehabilitator is a great way to get started and gain the experience necessary. You will learn how to handle and care for sick and injured wildlife, plus how to release animals safely back into the wild, raise funds, and manage a business.

When you are ready, you can obtain your permit and open a rehabilitation facility of your own. It is important to get proper training and experience. As a part of this job, you will encounter countless types of wildlife with unique and varied care needs. This is one job you cannot skimp on in regards to education.

Advertise your skills and services statewide. Wildlife rehabilitators often serve large areas because they are few and far between. By having a website and regularly posting in Facebook wildlife groups, you let people know who you are. Contact veterinarian offices. Oftentimes, people call the local veterinarian when finding injured wildlife.

Once you get a permit, you will be listed with Fish and Game in your state, so people can get your contact information from them when in need of your services.

There are many national organizations that you can volunteer with, as well. As you volunteer with an organization working with disasters, you may encounter various dangers, including hazardous materials. However, the organization will provide you with training before you begin.

Important Considerations

Wildlife may try to bite you because they terrified. They may also carry diseases and parasites. You must work in wildlife rehabilitation and gain experience to learn how to handle animals correctly and safely.

There are special techniques for handling all animals, from rabbits to birds to snakes. Never make the mistake and assume an animal is harmless! While animals don't mean harm, they instinctively act in self-defense, especially when they are hurt and afraid for their lives.

You cannot get personally attached to these animals. They are not meant to be pets. When they recover from an illness or injury, you will be releasing them back into the wild (if possible). This can be emotionally difficult for some people, but it is the ethical thing to do.

Wrap-Up

Working with wildlife is a unique experience and a way to make a positive difference in your environment and ecosystems. With many animals sick or injured, largely from human activities, your job will play a crucial role in helping these animals return to their habitats healthy again.

You will work closely with your community and state Fish and Game and/or U.S. Fish and Wildlife department to rescue and heal sick and injured birds, mammals, reptiles, amphibians, and more.

Now that you have read about various volunteer opportunities as well as in-person and online pet businesses you can start, you must learn how to handle the most important part of your business—your clients.

Your clients will be both animal and human, so you must

rehabilitation and gain experience to learn how to handle animals correctly and safely.

There are special techniques for handling all animals, from rabbits to birds to snakes. Never make the mistake and assume an animal is harmless! While animals don't mean harm, they instinctively act in self-defense, especially when they are hurt and afraid for their lives.

You cannot get personally attached to these animals. They are not meant to be pets. When they recover from an illness or injury, you will be releasing them back into the wild (if possible). This can be emotionally difficult for some people, but it is the ethical thing to do.

Wrap-Up

Working with wildlife is a unique experience and a way to make a positive difference in your environment and ecosystems. With many animals sick or injured, largely from human activities, your job will play a crucial role in helping these animals return to their habitats healthy again.

You will work closely with your community and state Fish and Game and/or U.S. Fish and Wildlife department to rescue and heal sick and injured birds, mammals, reptiles, amphibians, and more.

Now that you have read about various volunteer opportunities as well as in-person and online pet businesses you can start, you must learn how to handle the most important part of your business—your clients.

Your clients will be both animal and human, so you must

Working with an established wildlife rehabilitator is a great way to get started and gain the experience necessary. You will learn how to handle and care for sick and injured wildlife, plus how to release animals safely back into the wild, raise funds, and manage a business.

When you are ready, you can obtain your permit and open a rehabilitation facility of your own. It is important to get proper training and experience. As a part of this job, you will encounter countless types of wildlife with unique and varied care needs. This is one job you cannot skimp on in regards to education.

Advertise your skills and services statewide. Wildlife rehabilitators often serve large areas because they are few and far between. By having a website and regularly posting in Facebook wildlife groups, you let people know who you are. Contact veterinarian offices. Oftentimes, people call the local veterinarian when finding injured wildlife.

Once you get a permit, you will be listed with Fish and Game in your state, so people can get your contact information from them when in need of your services.

There are many national organizations that you can volunteer with, as well. As you volunteer with an organization working with disasters, you may encounter various dangers, including hazardous materials. However, the organization will provide you with training before you begin.

Important Considerations

Wildlife may try to bite you because they terrified. They may also carry diseases and parasites. You must work in wildlife

learn special skills for handling each. While pet businesses are fun and heartwarming for everyone involved, you may still encounter difficult clients of all species.

If you know how to handle them properly, you will get many happy repeat clients and great reviews that promote your business better than any other form of advertising.

However, before you move into the next section, go through the action steps to determine if a career (volunteer or paid) as a wildlife rehabilitator is for you.

Action Steps

1. Download your free gift. It contains links for schools and associations to get you started (Resources).
2. Do a search for local wildlife rehabilitators in your general area. Be prepared to drive, as many are located rurally.
3. When you find one that you feel is up to standards and meets your career goals, spend some time volunteering to determine if you enjoy this type of work and to learn the trade.
4. Consider taking courses that would increase your knowledge and efficiency.
5. Determine if you need to be licensed or certified to practice in your state.
6. Research appropriate licensing and permits needed to be a career rehabilitator or volunteer by reaching out to your state Fish and Game department or U.S. Fish and Wildlife.

7. List your information with Fish and Game, local veterinarians, and emergency veterinarian clinics.
8. Reach out to organizations that need wildlife rehabilitator volunteers if volunteering is your interest rather than a career.

7. List your information with Fish and Game, local veterinarians, and emergency veterinarian clinics.
8. Reach out to organizations that need wildlife rehabilitator volunteers if volunteering is your interest rather than a career.

learn special skills for handling each. While pet businesses are fun and heartwarming for everyone involved, you may still encounter difficult clients of all species.

If you know how to handle them properly, you will get many happy repeat clients and great reviews that promote your business better than any other form of advertising.

However, before you move into the next section, go through the action steps to determine if a career (volunteer or paid) as a wildlife rehabilitator is for you.

Action Steps

1. Download your free gift. It contains links for schools and associations to get you started (Resources).
2. Do a search for local wildlife rehabilitators in your general area. Be prepared to drive, as many are located rurally.
3. When you find one that you feel is up to standards and meets your career goals, spend some time volunteering to determine if you enjoy this type of work and to learn the trade.
4. Consider taking courses that would increase your knowledge and efficiency.
5. Determine if you need to be licensed or certified to practice in your state.
6. Research appropriate licensing and permits needed to be a career rehabilitator or volunteer by reaching out to your state Fish and Game department or U.S. Fish and Wildlife.

SECTION IV

JUMPSTART YOUR PET BUSINESS

Are you excited to get started? I am so excited for you! Starting a pet business is the key to making money doing something you love and enriching the lives of pets and their people alike.

In this section, I am going to cover ways to decide on your career by asking you to explore some important considerations. I am also going to help you get started with suggestions on business plans and financing.

Then there is creating your website and your brand. When you are in business, you must have a social presence so people can find and hire you. Without one, it could be nearly impossible to succeed.

Please read on to gain the knowledge necessary to start your own pet business.

SECTION IV

JUMPSTART YOUR PET BUSINESS

Are you excited to get started? I am so excited for you! Starting a pet business is the key to making money doing something you love and enriching the lives of pets and their people alike.

In this section, I am going to cover ways to decide on your career by asking you to explore some important considerations. I am also going to help you get started with suggestions on business plans and financing.

Then there is creating your website and your brand. When you are in business, you must have a social presence so people can find and hire you. Without one, it could be nearly impossible to succeed.

Please read on to gain the knowledge necessary to start your own pet business.

28

DECIDING WHAT YOU WANT TO DO

Have you decided what you want to do yet? Before you start your own pet business, you have to decide what kind of business to start. There are so many options in the pet industry, and this book is not able to cover all of them, though I do cover the most common ones and some uncommon choices.

Whether one of the job choices covered already speaks to you or you're still figuring that part out, you can benefit from considering business practices that will best fit your needs.

Let's get started!

Ideas

First of all, do you have an amazing idea for a business that I haven't covered? If you have a unique idea, then you already have an edge on your competition. You can corner the market and start a trend.

But not everyone has a fantastic, original idea for a pet business. That is still okay. You can enter an established line of work in the pet industry and still stand out. If you have a unique idea, however, you must market it because you are adding something to the world that no one has ever seen before.

Courage, Guts, and Strength

One thing all business owners in the world share is courage. It takes a lot of guts to try something despite the risks of failure. And it takes a lot of strength to leave behind a career you may already have to make your dreams come true.

But all business owners can agree—mustering the courage and opening your dream business is one hundred percent worth it. If your heart is in this, then you absolutely can do it. The fear that holds you back is not as important as the wonderful return you can get from a career you love.

Love for Animals

Have you ever taken your pet to a veterinarian or pet store where people clearly didn't like animals? You probably never went back! Yet, it warms your heart when you go into a place and the staff ooos and ahhs at your pet—telling her how cute she is.

To thrive in the pet industry, you must have a deep love of animals. Why go into an industry if you don't love it? That love will motivate you even when the going gets tough. You will actually want to go to work each morning—can you imagine that?

Support

Without a doubt, opening your own business is hard. You may have poor sales at first, or you may struggle with the start-up process. Having someone to support you is so important.

A partner or team in your business is always an amazing source of support. Having people you can trust to run your business with you is quite helpful and takes a load off of your shoulders.

At the very least, have someone who you can talk to about your trials and tribulations. A friend who listens can do you a world of good. You may also want to get to know other people in the pet industry who can give you advice.

Online or In Person

Do you want to work from home in your pajamas or handle pets in person? Some pet businesses, such as massage therapy (Chapter 16), are incompatible with the online format. Other ideas, like blogging (Chapter 1), can't be done in person. You have to choose whether you want to work from the computer or in a brick-and-mortar business.

Of course, many businesses can be split between online and in person. It is more than possible to run a small pet supply store and have an online store as well. You could be a veterinarian (Chapter 18) and write books (Check out my book, *Pet Authorpreneur 101: How to Become a Successful Pet Author and Grow Your Business* on Amazon) from home for pet people who care about the health of their beloved animals.

Time

Time is always a consideration. You must consider how much time you want to spend opening your business and how much time you want to spend working in your new pet career.

Many businesses take time to get started. Look at when you want to open the business. Then learn more about the time it takes to start to adjust your expectations realistically. If something takes too much time for you, you may want to consider a different business type.

How much do you want to work? Are you looking for a full-time business or a side gig? Some businesses are more than full time. As a veterinarian, you may be on call all of the time; as a store or kennel owner (Chapter 15), you may even have to work on days when you are closed, and you may not have much time for vacations.

Other businesses, such as pet writing, blogging, and animal communication (Chapter 3), are side gigs that you can do on top of other jobs or in retirement.

Education

Some of these careers require going back to school. To become a veterinarian, you need an advanced professional degree and up to four years of veterinarian school, on top of three to four years in undergraduate school. If you already have a degree in biology, zoology, or a similar field, you already have the undergraduate covered, but you are still looking at years of school and tuition. Don't let that discourage you—just consider it.

Veterinary technician (Chapter 19) often only requires an

associate's, which usually takes two years full-time. Other careers covered here may also require some schooling, such as massage therapy (Chapter 16) and energy healing (Chapter 14).

If you don't want to go back to school, that is okay. There are many options that don't require a special education. But going back to school to make your dream come true is always worthwhile. Don't let time or money discourage you from creating an amazing career.

Initial Investment

Another important consideration is your initial investment when starting your business. Like all businesses, you have to spend some money to make money. Consider your budget and what you can spend to launch a pet career.

Some businesses have start-up costs that are much higher than others when you consider tuition, licensing, inventory, etc.

Other careers, such as pet blogging (Chapter 1), only cost as much as your website and your time. Depending on the hosting service you pick and the theme you use, your start-up costs can be quite small, less than a thousand per year.

Create a To-Do List

The actual first step is creating a to-do list. It is going to be quite long at first, but as you check items off, your confidence and sense of accomplishment will soar. Begin to read the section of this book that applies to your chosen job and then add each action item to a to-do list. Check it off once it is accomplished.

Here are a few items that will be on your to-do list. I will cover them in more detail in the next chapter:

- Research
- Develop a business plan
- Procure funding if you don't have enough money to start the business
- Find a space
- Start a website
- Fund advertising

Wrap-Up

In this chapter, you have learned that starting a career in the pet industry can be very rewarding. You also learned how important it is to follow your heart and nurture your love of animals to create a dream job.

There are a number of factors that you must consider to find the business that best fits your needs. Starting any kind of business or new job takes time, money, and effort. Be sure to use your inspiration to fuel your motivation.

Use the action steps at the end of this chapter to get you started with finding your direction and being honest with all the considerations this book has presented to you.

Now, read on to learn more about the steps to launching your own business. In Chapter 29, I will cover developing your business plan, marketing and sales, funding, finding a space, developing your brand, creating a website, and more.

Action Steps

1. Make a list of all the considerations outlined in this chapter.
2. Under each consideration, add your thoughts, feelings, and inspirations as it pertains to your life and goals.
3. Start writing a preliminary to-do list to make your dream happen.
4. Stay focused, believe in yourself, and know you can excel with your dream job.

29

GETTING STARTED

Do you have a specific niche in the pet industry in mind, and are you are ready to get started? You just need to start researching your niche and figuring out what to do first.

Using this book, you can learn everything you need to get started. But you may also have to look into your local prices, business licensing practices, and labor laws to start your business—especially if you are opening a storefront business. You may also have to research funding sources.

Start Your Research

The first place to start is online. Look at other businesses in your area if you are starting a storefront business. If you are starting an online business, research your competitors and influencers.

Look at their business practices, prices, and even statistics from the Department of Labor (storefront). All of this can be useful for learning about the industry and what you can expect in your area.

You can also visit your library. You can learn about real estate rates, the history of businesses, and other such information there. View public records to see how pet businesses in your area are faring.

Contact your local chamber of commerce to learn about how to proceed with legally opening a storefront business. You want to find out about any necessary licenses and permits. You also want to learn about applicable taxes.

Get the appropriate paperwork to begin the process of opening a legal business. Add any costs you learn about to your budget. With an online business, you don't need to do this step.

If you are entering a career that calls for schooling, research schools. Contact admissions for information about how to get started, estimated costs of attendance, and the time needed to complete a degree. You may want to go on college tours to find out where you want to attend. Visiting a campus in person lets you get a much better feel for its culture and whether or not it is right for you.

Talk to pet business owners, both online and storefront. Some of these owners may not be willing to talk to future competition, but some are more than amicable to the idea of helping others and expanding the pet industry.

You may even meet people interested in hiring you, working for you, supporting your business, entering an affiliate partnership with you, or going into business with you somehow.

Networking is key to business because you never know what opportunities other people have for you.

Reach out to pet business owners in your niche and politely introduce yourself. Disclose why you are contacting them and ask, "Would you be willing to help me?" Then ask them how they started the business, how they fare in different economic times, and other such questions.

Develop a Business Plan

Whether you are starting an online or storefront business—and before you procure a loan or get a business license—you must have a business plan in place. If this part is overwhelming for you, consider hiring someone to help you. SCORE (Resources) is a free resource. You can find them by going to score.org.

Your business plan has to reflect what your business is, what your business provides, how much your start-up costs are expected to be, and what you plan to do with all funding.

It should also reflect what you expect to make. While you may not know exactly what these figures are, you can find a projected estimate of profits by researching similar businesses in your area or online. If there are few businesses like yours in your area, you may still thrive, but you look like a risk to potential investors.

Using the information from your research, start to devise a plan. To learn about business structure, you can download free business plan templates online or get help from SCORE.

A business plan must include:

Executive Summary

The executive summary is quite simple—it describes the information covered under the headings mentioned in this chapter in one paragraph. This is a succinct way to break down the information of your business plan for any person who will be reading it. You place the executive summary on top of your document.

There is no need for flowery words and long sentences. Someone who is not interested in your business will not waste any more time on the plan after reading the summary; someone who is interested will be intrigued enough to read on.

Next, you want to provide more detail with each of the headings mentioned in this chapter. This information will be presented under the executive summary.

Company Profile

First, describe your company. Talk about:

- what kind of business you are opening
- the products/services you are offering
- your mission to make a difference in your community or the world
- the history of your company
- any resources you have
- the types of animals and people you will serve

- what makes your business unique from others

This part needs to be clear. But it also can be a bit more detailed than your executive summary. Basically, you want to give someone a very good feel for the company you are founding. Once you write this profile, you can reuse it on your "About" pages online.

Market Analysis

This is where your research comes in handy. You want to show that you know your market well. Show the statistics for your type of business, the gains and losses you anticipate, and the way you have licensed or will license your business. Describe your location and how it will serve your business. Document your anticipated cash flow and expenses based on what other businesses in your niche make.

Business Structure

First, what will your role in the business be? Do you have any partners? Will you have employees? Describe how the business will be run and how you will hire employees. Describe the roles and ranks of these employees.

You also want to describe how you plan to run this business. For instance, if you're running a kennel, will you be boarding the dogs in your home? Do you have a big yard?

Services and Products

This part is easy enough. All you have to do is list the kinds of services and products you are going to sell. Describe each in brief detail and add how much you plan to charge. Also, describe the ingredients of the products and how they are unique from what other people offer.

Marketing and Sales

Describe how you plan to sell your products or services. In detail, go into the kinds of advertising and marketing you will use. Discuss how you plan to reach people. You may also mention things like sales or specials you will use to boost sales. The point here is to prove how you plan to make money.

You want to go into a lot of detail here. Don't just say, "I will host spring sales." Instead, describe how you will bundle products, offer up to fifty percent off, and other such deals in spring every year.

Funding Request

When obtaining a loan or investment, you want to include a formal request for the money you need. You want to describe how much money you need, where that money will go, and how you will benefit from it. You also want to describe the sort of return the bank or investor can expect.

This request can be tailored to each person. Write it as if you are addressing the person you give your business plan to personally. You may even write it as a letter, starting with "Dear [reader's name]" and ending with "Sincerely, [your name]." Include formal language and ask, "Please consider providing funding to this venture."

Financial Projections

To get any sort of investment or loan, you have to prove that your business will return the money others have given you. You want to use your marketing analysis to predict how much money you will make. Then describe how you can pay off loans or return investments with this profit. This part will read similar to a college dissertation.

I highly recommend hiring an accountant if you need help with this part. Determining investments and loans can be extremely intimidating if you are not good with numbers. If you cannot afford an accountant, SCORE will offer help with this. Or you can maybe barter with an accountant with services from your new business!

Procure Funding

If you have enough money to launch your business, that is awesome! You can dip into savings or use a second job to help fund a business. But if you don't have the money, don't despair. There are ways you can procure funding from other sources.

The first way is to obtain a loan from a family member or friend. If you can get someone to lend you the money, you may be able to avoid the high interest rates some banks may have. If no one can give you a personal loan, you can approach banks for a small business loan. Show the bank your business plan and your plan to pay the loan back.

You may approach investors. Investors are people who will give you money and expect some sort of financial return. They may buy a percentage of your company, for example. Approach businesspeople in your area and ask if they are interested in investing. Pitch your company and how it will make them money, and show them your business plan. The point here is to prove to investors how they will benefit.

You may also get someone to go into business with you. You will have to share a part of your company with this person and give this person certain responsibilities and privileges. However, this person can provide you with financial and business support. A good partner would be someone who has already worked in the pet industry and has some know-how.

Find a Space

If you are running a business that is in person (See Section II), then you will need a space. You may rent a commercial space, or you may run the business out of your home. You must obtain appropriate permits for either, and then you must rent or buy the space, set up the space with appropriate equipment, and pass inspection in most states.

Start by visiting your local chamber of commerce and learning what you must do to get a space approved within your city and state. Adjust your business plan accordingly. Some cities have ordinances that don't allow you to operate businesses from inside your residence—for instance, if your business plan involves starting a home-based business, you may have to edit that.

Next, contact real estate offices in your area to find a commercial real estate agent. Discuss your budget and needs with the agent and tour some available commercial spaces. Lease or purchase the one you like the most.

Once your space passes state inspection, you can start to set it up according to your needs. Get the equipment you need. Install any special plumbing or wiring necessary. For a grooming business, for example, you may want to install special sinks and floor drains. For a pet bakery, you will need to install display cases and ovens. For a store, you need racks and display cases and a counter for a cash register.

Keep in mind, for an online business, you do not need to do this. What you do need to consider is your home workspace. Do you have a place in your home to set up your computer? Is it large enough for your needs? Do you have appropriate Internet service to handle your work?

Build a Web Presence

In this modern age, you cannot have a business without a website. You must have a web presence, whether your business is online or not. Fortunately, a website is fairly cheap. Please see Chapter 30 for how to build one.

Also create social media accounts separate from personal accounts for your business. You want to feature yourself on Instagram, Facebook, Twitter, LinkedIn, and other popular social media sites that may arise with the times.

On these accounts, feature a profile describing your business, mission, and vision.

cial real estate agent. Discuss your budget and needs with the agent and tour some available commercial spaces. Lease or purchase the one you like the most.

Once your space passes state inspection, you can start to set it up according to your needs. Get the equipment you need. Install any special plumbing or wiring necessary. For a grooming business, for example, you may want to install special sinks and floor drains. For a pet bakery, you will need to install display cases and ovens. For a store, you need racks and display cases and a counter for a cash register.

Keep in mind, for an online business, you do not need to do this. What you do need to consider is your home workspace. Do you have a place in your home to set up your computer? Is it large enough for your needs? Do you have appropriate Internet service to handle your work?

Build a Web Presence

In this modern age, you cannot have a business without a website. You must have a web presence, whether your business is online or not. Fortunately, a website is fairly cheap. Please see Chapter 30 for how to build one.

Also create social media accounts separate from personal accounts for your business. You want to feature yourself on Instagram, Facebook, Twitter, LinkedIn, and other popular social media sites that may arise with the times.

On these accounts, feature a profile describing your business, mission, and vision.

You may approach investors. Investors are people who will give you money and expect some sort of financial return. They may buy a percentage of your company, for example. Approach businesspeople in your area and ask if they are interested in investing. Pitch your company and how it will make them money, and show them your business plan. The point here is to prove to investors how they will benefit.

You may also get someone to go into business with you. You will have to share a part of your company with this person and give this person certain responsibilities and privileges. However, this person can provide you with financial and business support. A good partner would be someone who has already worked in the pet industry and has some know-how.

Find a Space

If you are running a business that is in person (See Section II), then you will need a space. You may rent a commercial space, or you may run the business out of your home. You must obtain appropriate permits for either, and then you must rent or buy the space, set up the space with appropriate equipment, and pass inspection in most states.

Start by visiting your local chamber of commerce and learning what you must do to get a space approved within your city and state. Adjust your business plan accordingly. Some cities have ordinances that don't allow you to operate businesses from inside your residence—for instance, if your business plan involves starting a home-based business, you may have to edit that.

Next, contact real estate offices in your area to find a commer-

- Have your logo or a cute picture representing your business as your profile picture.
- Feature pictures of your products and services; for example, as a dog groomer, you want a portfolio of some of your best grooming jobs.
- Also feature a link to your website.
- Post business hours in your about me section.
- Make it easy for people to access your online store and contact you.

For a small fee, you can purchase Facebook advertising, which will get you more followers. You can also get followers by posting frequently in groups related to your business.

Frequently post on your accounts about new products, specials, or jobs to engage with followers. Always answer messages as soon as you can. I recommend setting aside a certain amount of time each day to answer correspondence from social media and your website.

Finally, post a listing on Yelp, among other local business sites, if you are opening a storefront. You can register on these sites for free at Yelp.com. This lets potential customers find you online if they search for your type of business. You want to post your hours, your location, your phone number, and your website.

Also, post a picture of your business and use your logo for your profile picture. The registration is free, but you can also purchase advertising for a small fee that lets the site you are registered on put you in front of more customers.

Advertise

You can run the best business in the world, but you won't get any customers if they don't know you exist! You have to put yourself out there. That's why you should budget a few hundred to a few thousand a year for advertising, or at least seven percent of your revenue. It will be worth it!

Get Business Cards

The first thing you should do is order business cards. Vistaprint (Resources) and Shutterfly (Resources) are great places to get affordable, professional-looking business cards. Make the cards simple—your business name, hours, website, phone number, email, and logo.

On the back, you can write something personal, such as "Can't wait to meet you and your beloved companion!" This is a nice touch that makes an even better impression on potential customers. I have found that bright colors and cute logos of pets are often more attractive to customers in the pet industry.

You can also use Vistaprint or Shutterfly to print T-shirts, flyers, and signs for your business. Also, look into local businesses to do your printing and build your network of supporters. If you are running your business out of your home, consider a sign to put on your lawn to advertise what you offer.

Create a Logo

You might be wondering how to create a logo. Fortunately, you don't need to be an artist to accomplish that. Simply visit

PicMonkey (Resources), a graphic design site. There, you can use the tools to create a logo.

You can also search on Fiverr.com (Resources) to find logo makers and graphic designers. Freelance sites like Guru.com and Upwork.com (Resources) often have many graphic designers looking for jobs. Hire someone whose portfolio matches what you are looking for. Make your specifications clear.

Your logo doesn't have to be fancy. My logo for CenterForPetLossGrief.com is a classic example of a simple logo that is instantly recognizable. Have your logo feature a pet that your business serves or a group of animals. Use bright colors to attract people's attention if appropriate for you niche. If you can, incorporate the name. When you don't have any ideas for how to do this, just hire someone and have them propose a few different logo ideas.

Once you have your logo, you have a symbol that makes your business instantly recognizable. You can post it on your website, your social media accounts, and your business advertising. Be sure to include it on your business cards.

Advertising Options

You can start by using online advertising. Facebook, Instagram, and Yelp all have great advertising options that cost very little. You can explore other online options as well. Promote your web presence, especially if you are an online business.

You should also consider a radio ad. Radio ads are fairly expensive, but they bring in twice as much traffic! Contact your local radio station to find out rates. Often, they will help you record your ad. Then they will play it as often as your package specifies. TV ads are also an option, but they can run very high costs.

Your local newspaper is a great place to post a weekly classified ad for your business if you are locally based. Contact local papers and find out their rates. Create a small ad featuring your business name, logo, and slogan, and run it every week.

Ask your local chamber of commerce about places to post signs for your business. Often, the chamber of commerce itself will have a board where you can pin your sign or business card. That's free advertising right there.

You can also advertise at other related businesses. For instance, if you are a pet groomer or photographer, you can post a sign at your local shelters, pet stores, and boarding kennels (with the owners' permission, of course). Or if you run a boarding kennel, post a sign or offer a stack of cards at all local groomers, shelters, and pet stores. Don't try to advertise at a competitor's business, as that usually won't go over well!

Sometimes, you have to advertise in person. I know a woman who runs an at-home doggie day care. She likes to stand at local festivals and events and hand out her business cards. She gets a lot of business this way. By being present at events and handing out cards or hosting a booth, you get to interact with people and make a great impression that sticks with them.

Finally, be sure to utilize signage. If you are opening a brick-and-mortar business, post your name as soon as you have your space. Place a banner advertising your business and announcing when you will open in the window or over the door.

On the first week of business, have a large "Grand Opening" sign. Signage attracts lots of vehicle and foot traffic. Of course, this does not apply to strictly online businesses.

Wrap-Up

You have learned how to hone in on the development, purpose, and future of your new business. Your to-do list may seem long at first, but as you tackle each item, you will feel more and more invigorated!

Making your dream business or career happen is no easy feat, but it is completely worth it. Take some time to start research and draft your business plan, if necessary. Research and visit schools if you want to go back to school. Then, read on to learn how to create a website and go into your desired field.

Use the action steps at the end of this chapter to help you do the necessary research and development. This step is necessary whether you are starting an online or storefront business.

In Chapter 30, you will learn about creating your website, which is imperative for every kind of business. Your website lets you define who you are. It also is a form of affordable advertising.

Action Steps

1. If you are opening a storefront business, reach out to five local businesses and introduce yourself and your new business. If you are starting an online business, reach out to five influencers in your niche.

2. Create a business plan. Tailor it for each person who will see it.
3. Get funding through partnerships, investors, and loans.
4. If you are starting an in-person business, rent or buy a space.
5. Develop your web presence. You want to create a website and social media accounts, even if your business is not online.
6. Advertise!! You want to let people know that you exist. Do it online and in person. Use a logo. Print business cards.
7. If any of these steps are overwhelming, get help from SCORE or business owners that would be willing to give you advice.

30

CREATING YOUR WEBSITE

Would you like to get away with not having a website for your business? Well, I hate to disappoint you…but you absolutely must have a website to go with your business.

If the idea of starting a website makes you shudder in horror, never fear! You can either hire a great web designer to create one for you or you can read my book, *Pet Blogging 101: How to Start a Riveting Pet Blog and Gain Loyal Followers* and find out how to create one yourself for very little money.

In this chapter, I am going to cover what goes into creating your website to gain loyal followers and customers. Please read on to learn why a website is important and what content you should include.

People Find You With a Website

First, a website is important because it helps people find you. Say you own a grooming shop. Someone just moved to your area, and they don't know where to go for their grooming needs.

Because most folks rely heavily on the Internet, this person will probably look up grooming shops in the area and find your site. When they call you and visit your shop, you potentially earned a new customer! If you are not online, however, this new customer will go to a competitor who is. You just missed out.

Having a web presence lets people know who you are, what you offer, and where you are located. Since people often use iPads and smartphones to find local businesses or order products, you should have a website they can easily find on all devices—not just on a computer.

Consider having listings with Yelp and Google so people can find out about your business when they are looking for local places. Make it easy for people to contact you by including links to your website, phone number, address, and hours.

With a website, you can advertise yourself fairly cheaply. You can pay for advertising in a variety of places so your website and business are placed in front of people. This is cheaper than most other forms of advertising, and it reaches more people, since people are often online.

Furthermore, if you are an online business, no one will find you unless you rank highly in searches and have ads. You need to have a website so people can access your products or services. You also need to optimize (Glossary) your website. When people search for their pet needs, your site pops up and provides what they are looking for.

A Website Defines Your Business

A website lets you express yourself and show people who you are as a business. Someone may drive by your grooming shop or boarding kennel and think, "I want to check that place out!" They do an online search and find out about your history, your deep love of pets, and how you like to do business. They see testimonials and reviews attesting to how awesome you are. So… they are inclined to do business with you! See why this is so important?

Now imagine the opposite scenario. Have you ever driven past a place and want to find out more about it, yet when you search online, you find no website and a disconnected phone number on the Yelp listing? This has happened to me before, and I lost interest in the place of business as a result. You don't want to lose customers just because you're not accessible online.

With your website, you can show people what you are about and what you do—your brand. You can showcase your skills or products and reviews. Then, people feel like they know you and want to take a chance on you. They know what to expect when they walk into your place of business or click through your site. A sense of trust is forged long before they even meet you.

Realize that entering your business or calling you personally takes a time investment for people. They won't do it if they don't already have an idea that they want to do business with you. Your website helps you prove your business is worth the time investment.

Wrap-Up

A professional website is a necessary business choice when you want to stay in communication with your customers and clients. Whether you have a storefront or online business, creating your website allows you to build a following of loyal customers and alert them with important updates and announcements.

The action steps at the end of this chapter will help you begin thinking about your website. This step is necessary whether you are starting an online or storefront business.

In Chapter 31, you will learn the steps needed to create your website.

Action Steps

1. Make a list of why you think your business needs a website. Try to think of different ideas than the ones already discussed in this chapter.
2. Create another list that includes five needs your customers may have. Interview friends, family, current clients, and potential clients.
3. Complete the list you made for number two by adding to your list the solutions you have for your customers. You want to have solutions for their five needs that you will provide for them.
4. With each solution, write a short three- to four-line paragraph on how you are going to solve their issue

31

DEVELOPING YOUR WEBSITE

Are you feeling overwhelmed with the idea of creating a website? No worries…I am going to teach you what goes into a website so your business can thrive.

I can't stress enough how important it is to spend time developing your brand (Glossary) and website. If you rush through this step, your website will not accurately reflect the business you do. Business is then lost.

In this chapter, you will learn how to organize and develop the content that goes into your site. Developing and creating a website is a fun project. In fact, it is one of my favorite tasks when helping people create a pet business. Take the time to make your business personable and stand out to gain those loyal customers who keep coming back for more.

What Your Website Should Include:

Company Profile

First and foremost, your website must include a company profile. This is a page where you talk about you and your staff. You mention the things your business sells and how you help animals and their people. You also talk a bit about your history and your inspiration for creating the business.

The company profile is essential because it lets people know if their values align with yours and if your business can meet their needs. You want to be very clear with the services and products you offer to help your customers solve their needs—remember the work you did in Chapters 28, 29, and 30?

When you make it easy for your website visitors to understand what you do to help them, you have easily gained a new customer or client. However, if you are vague and not sure exactly what you offer, it becomes confusing for them, and they won't go past the first page.

Contact Page

Always have a page with a contact form. Once someone submits the form, you should receive it through your contact form widget (Glossary). The contact form should include a way to get back to the person as well as the subject and message of their trouble or question.

In addition to this form, you should post your business hours, address, and phone. That way people can reach you in a variety of ways. Also offer your social media links.

Company Profile

First and foremost, your website must include a company profile. This is a page where you talk about you and your staff. You mention the things your business sells and how you help animals and their people. You also talk a bit about your history and your inspiration for creating the business.

The company profile is essential because it lets people know if their values align with yours and if your business can meet their needs. You want to be very clear with the services and products you offer to help your customers solve their needs—remember the work you did in Chapters 28, 29, and 30?

When you make it easy for your website visitors to understand what you do to help them, you have easily gained a new customer or client. However, if you are vague and not sure exactly what you offer, it becomes confusing for them, and they won't go past the first page.

Contact Page

Always have a page with a contact form. Once someone submits the form, you should receive it through your contact form widget (Glossary). The contact form should include a way to get back to the person as well as the subject and message of their trouble or question.

In addition to this form, you should post your business hours, address, and phone. That way people can reach you in a variety of ways. Also offer your social media links.

31

DEVELOPING YOUR WEBSITE

Are you feeling overwhelmed with the idea of creating a website? No worries…I am going to teach you what goes into a website so your business can thrive.

I can't stress enough how important it is to spend time developing your brand (Glossary) and website. If you rush through this step, your website will not accurately reflect the business you do. Business is then lost.

In this chapter, you will learn how to organize and develop the content that goes into your site. Developing and creating a website is a fun project. In fact, it is one of my favorite tasks when helping people create a pet business. Take the time to make your business personable and stand out to gain those loyal customers who keep coming back for more.

What Your Website Should Include:

Store

It's always a good idea to offer a store on your website showing what products you carry. Even if you don't want to sell things online, having an online showcase of what your storefront business offers can help people see if you carry what they are looking for before they come by your place of business. Include descriptions and photos of the products you carry.

That said, I would strongly consider supporting online ordering. People are relying more on this method to obtain the products they need more than ever before.

Services

If you are in a service industry, include a page outlining the different services you offer. You want to include as many details as possible so people have fewer questions.

In Chapter 30, you outlined the needs of your clients and the solutions you offer to help them. This page is a perfect place to state those needs and solutions again to remind your potential new client.

Offer a contact form at the bottom of the page so that people can conveniently reach you with questions or a place for people to book a service with you. These little thoughtful things make people like your business more and thus encourage them to seek your business out when they need help!

Portfolio

Show off your artwork, grooming, photography, or T-shirt designs with a portfolio. Showcase your best work to prove to people that they should hire you. Let people get a sense of your style so that they know what to expect and if you are the right fit for their wants.

Your portfolio must include photos that are high resolution, well lit, and flattering. A grainy, dim photo can't show off your work. Be sure to crop the photos or take them against a white or black background so there is no clutter or distractions in them. Also be sure to include the entire item, not just a small part. A watermark can help you prevent image theft.

Quotes and a Booking Service

A lot of people love the convenience of getting a price quote and booking a service online. If you are in any sort of pet service industry, make it easy and convenient by offering a booking button under each listed service and a form for requesting or generating quotes. Make sure you also offer a contact form on this page so that you can get back to a customer with a quote.

Reviews/Testimonials

The only way potential customers know to trust your business is by reading the experiences of other people. By providing a page for reviews and real testimonials, you make it easy for word-of-mouth advertising. Dedicate a page to reviews and have a form so people can post them. Encourage customers to leave you reviews and tell them how much it will help you out!

Ask permission from your reviewers to use their picture and full name. This way the testimonial looks professional, credible, and personal.

On Facebook, Google, and Yelp, people can also leave reviews after they visit your business. Customize these listings with your hours and contact information and link to your website. That way, people can easily find you and your reviews in one place when they look up local businesses. To reach more people, expand the area your listing serves to include nearby towns.

Blog

Even if you don't want to make money as a pet blogger, hosting a blog on your site can be very helpful to your business. To get started, my book, *Pet Blogging 101: How to Start a Riveting Pet Blog and Gain Loyal Followers,* will help you every step of the way.

A blog can help you teach people information about your products, or share valuable insights with pet owners, or simply make pet lovers smile as you share cute stories and photos of your own beloved animals.

A blog gives you a medium to communicate with your customers. It lets you express who you are and who your company is. Finally, it creates discussion and interaction with your customers and readers. People will get a good feel for you through your blog.

Social Media Links

You must create accounts on all of the popular social media sites for your business. Then, post links to each in the form of handy buttons on the bottom of each page of your site. That way, people can easily follow you and stay in touch with you.

Social media helps visitors learn about new posts, new services, new products, and other news through your social media posts. It can be a lot easier to reach people through social media posts than email lists that may go to spam or posts on your site that people may not see.

Once you are present on social media, be sure to stay active—post regularly. Some software plug-ins make posts on a schedule for you. The more you post, the more people feel engaged with you. You will attract and keep followers. You can post things that talk about your business or illustrate your opinions so that people know more about your business.

Also, take advantage of the ad programs offered on some sites like Facebook and Instagram. The ad programs can be profitable. However, there is a learning curve to ads.

Finally, when people comment on your social media posts or contact you—be sure to answer them. This helps with your reputation as a trusted pet business owner.

Collect Emails

When people visit your website, have a place allowing them to sign up for your email list. Include a sign-up link on every page.

You can send people on your email list newsletters that talk about your business, advertise new products, or alert people to important information they should know about. This keeps people aware of your business and helps you stay relevant to their needs.

Wrap-Up

A website is imperative for any kind of business. Not only does it define your business, but it lets people know who you are. For online businesses, your website is the epicenter of your business. Websites are a place for you to advertise and promote yourself—they give you the means to connect with people worldwide.

In today's Internet Age, you can make a lot of money working online from the comfort of your home. In fact, you may do even better than brick-and-mortar businesses. You can also cut down on overhead costs like space rental with an online business. The Internet has many opportunities, so be sure to take advantage of it!

After you complete your action steps for this chapter, read on to learn about some important customer service tips in Section V. I have been in business for a long time and can share countless stories. My goal in the next chapter is to prepare you so that you may avoid some unnecessary issues.

Action Steps

1. Start brainstorming your website with the

components I listed above. Not all of them will be appropriate for your business, but many of them will.
2. Learn how to build your website with my first book, *Pet Blogging 101: How to Start a Riveting Pet Blog and Gain Loyal Followers.*
3. Hire someone if you don't want to do it yourself. Websites can be tricky, so if you are hesitant to try, just find someone that has experience.
4. Remember to post your company profile.
5. Include an easy way to contact you.
6. Showcase your items or services or art.
7. Post all reviews and make it possible for people to add reviews.
8. Write a blog so you can be found by the search engines (Glossary).
9. Collect emails and send newsletters to people on your email list.
10. Include social media links. Always have social media accounts and update regularly.

SECTION V

CUSTOMER SERVICE TIPS

Are you a people pleaser? And are you wondering why I didn't ask if you were an animal pleaser?

Well…you probably already love animals. And you know how to do great things for them. However, their sometimes not-so-cute owners can be extremely challenging. Plus, sometimes those cute animals are scared—they can, and will, bite!

How can you handle difficult customers and clients plus still have passion for what you do?

In this section, I am going to cover how to:

1. Handle animals that are fearful, stressed out, and possibly aggressive.
2. Handle people that are rude, nasty, and a pain in the $*#! with grace.

3. Get your clients to keep coming back for your services and more!

32

HANDLING AGGRESSIVE AND DIFFICULT ANIMALS

Do you know why an animal is being aggressive or difficult? Probably because he or she is scared. Some dogs (and other animals) may not be socialized well and are terrified when handled by someone other than their people. They can lash out by biting in self-defense.

Cats and birds are particularly known for becoming scared and agitated when they are taken out of their element. Depending on your pet career, you may encounter animals who are petrified, freaked out, and feel trapped.

Furthermore, you may not have an animal's full history. Some pets may have been traumatized. You may have a dog become afraid of you if you wear a hat. Someone who always wore a hat may have abused this dog.

You also don't know how a pet has been trained or socialized. Some animals have not been raised to be friendly to others, and thus they pose significant challenges to pet industry workers who handle them.

The first step is to watch any animal you work with closely. Even a friendly, likeable pet may become scared at any moment. Maybe you are a groomer and you approach an area of a dog's body that he doesn't want you to touch. That sweet dog will turn into a snapping wild animal in a matter of milliseconds. Be on your guard at all times.

Once when I was giving a massage to a quarter horse, I touched a sore point on his back. He almost kicked me in the head. It was a good thing I was paying attention because I was able to jump out of the way just in time.

Animals give clues to their emotional state with their body language. A cat might pin its ears back and switch its tail in short, rapid strokes. A dog might pin its ears back or point them sharply forward, lower its head, and show its gums. Learn the warning signs for different kinds of animals.

Never trust an owner who insists, "He's friendly." Or, "She won't bite." Even if you have worked with the animal before—or the owner says he or she is nice—you never know what may send him into scared mode. Be equally cautious with all animals you work with.

Here Are Some General Points to Follow:

- Have a firm but gentle and calm approach.
- Try to keep their person around if they are calm. If not, ask them to leave the room.
- Encourage the person to hold the pet as you

introduce yourself to him or her, if appropriate. This can make an animal either more nervous or can let the animal know the owner thinks you are okay. Hopefully, this will set him or her at ease.
- Talk to the pet and let him or her smell you, if applicable.
- Spend a few minutes getting to know each other.
- Move around him or her firmly and deliberately—talk to him or her the entire time.
- When you touch him or her, start slowly and gently.
- Don't try and trick any nervous pet, as he or she can sense your behavior. I promise you it will make him or her more nervous.

Many veterinarians report they like to tell the pet what they are going to do. The veterinarian's confidence and reassuring tone helps set the pet's nerves at ease. Try this approach and talk to the pet you are handling.

If the owner is okay with it, you can offer their companion a treat. This further lets him or her know you don't mean harm. When a pet associates you with food, he or she may not fall in love with you, but he or she will think, "This person is safe and will not harm me."

Don't be afraid to employ restraint systems or muzzles if need be. If the owner does not like it, show him or her how the system is not meant to hurt animals and explain why you use it.

Groomers and veterinarians will sometimes use a humane restraint system that keeps an animal from biting—if needed. Also, protect yourself from bites, scratches, and diseases with gloves and protective clothing appropriate to your profession.

Wrap-Up

We all love animals. But sometimes our favorite animal clients can become difficult when they become afraid or sense they are being threatened. Since your profession may expose a pet to a new environment and new people, the pet's sense of nervousness will be heightened. You can take steps to minimize bad experiences for the animals you work with.

Our animal clients are not always our most difficult. Sometimes, people can prove to be much more troublesome. Read on to learn how to mitigate problems with your human clients after you do the action steps for this chapter.

Action Steps

1. Watch a pet closely for signs of potential stress, fear, etc.
2. Be gentle but firm—move with confidence.
3. Tell pets what you are going to do with a calm voice. They find your voice soothing.
4. Appease the pet and provide treats. Have the owner calm the pet, if possible—and only if they are not making the animal more uncomfortable. If they are, ask them kindly to leave the room for the animal's safety.
5. Use safety measures like restraint systems and gloves, if needed. Introduce them to the animal slowly.

diseases with gloves and protective clothing appropriate to your profession.

Wrap-Up

We all love animals. But sometimes our favorite animal clients can become difficult when they become afraid or sense they are being threatened. Since your profession may expose a pet to a new environment and new people, the pet's sense of nervousness will be heightened. You can take steps to minimize bad experiences for the animals you work with.

Our animal clients are not always our most difficult. Sometimes, people can prove to be much more troublesome. Read on to learn how to mitigate problems with your human clients after you do the action steps for this chapter.

Action Steps

1. Watch a pet closely for signs of potential stress, fear, etc.
2. Be gentle but firm—move with confidence.
3. Tell pets what you are going to do with a calm voice. They find your voice soothing.
4. Appease the pet and provide treats. Have the owner calm the pet, if possible—and only if they are not making the animal more uncomfortable. If they are, ask them kindly to leave the room for the animal's safety.
5. Use safety measures like restraint systems and gloves, if needed. Introduce them to the animal slowly.

introduce yourself to him or her, if appropriate. This can make an animal either more nervous or can let the animal know the owner thinks you are okay. Hopefully, this will set him or her at ease.
- Talk to the pet and let him or her smell you, if applicable.
- Spend a few minutes getting to know each other.
- Move around him or her firmly and deliberately—talk to him or her the entire time.
- When you touch him or her, start slowly and gently.
- Don't try and trick any nervous pet, as he or she can sense your behavior. I promise you it will make him or her more nervous.

Many veterinarians report they like to tell the pet what they are going to do. The veterinarian's confidence and reassuring tone helps set the pet's nerves at ease. Try this approach and talk to the pet you are handling.

If the owner is okay with it, you can offer their companion a treat. This further lets him or her know you don't mean harm. When a pet associates you with food, he or she may not fall in love with you, but he or she will think, "This person is safe and will not harm me."

Don't be afraid to employ restraint systems or muzzles if need be. If the owner does not like it, show him or her how the system is not meant to hurt animals and explain why you use it.

Groomers and veterinarians will sometimes use a humane restraint system that keeps an animal from biting—if needed. Also, protect yourself from bites, scratches, and

Pet Jobs 101

33

HANDLING DIFFICULT PEOPLE

Are you worried about handling demanding people? I must say that pet owners are wonderful people. But anyone who has worked in any kind of customer service (which is what any pet business involves) can tell you some people are just difficult.

The human component of the pet industry is definitely something you have to contend with. The pets may be great, but the owners, not so much.

Here are a few things to consider:

1. Pet people have high expectations, and you must be willing to meet them.
2. You must treat your customers well or they will feel unappreciated and refuse to use your business in the future.

3. If they are not happy with your service, they will leave bad reviews and tell other people not to use your services or products. That can majorly hurt your bottom line.
4. Even reasonable and levelheaded people can become belligerent and overprotective out of sheer worry for their pets' safety.
5. You must brush up on your customer service skills even if you prefer animals over people.

Calming Angry Clients

When someone is berating you, it is easy to begin crying or yelling, depending on your temperament. You must keep a smile on your face, and you must speak clearly, gently, and politely at all times. There is no room for sarcasm, yelling, or other such behavior when you are a business owner—even if some clients deserve it!

It is only human to react when someone is being difficult. Becoming defensive is natural to any person. But you must train yourself to ignore the impulse to become defensive when someone attacks you as a business owner.

Arguing will only provoke the angry person. Instead, smile, listen, and then ask what you can do to help. And *never* tell a client he or she is wrong—even if he or she is—because that will only infuriate the client more.

In some cases, it is necessary to apologize. Only apologize when you have actually done something wrong, like send the wrong product or charge a customer incorrectly. Say, "I'm so sorry. How can I resolve this issue for you and make things right?" Let the customer come up with a solution. This will start to defuse the customer's anger and let him or her feel as if you are actively trying to solve the problem at hand. It also makes the customer feel valued.

Listen to what your customer wants. By calmly asking questions about the issue, you can get a better picture of the problem and how to handle it. You also force the customer to calm down as he or she has to answer questions and provide information. Using "we" terms, invite collaboration with the customer:

"I am sorry this happened. We can certainly make this problem right. How do you feel about an exchange?" is an example of doing this. Or you could say, "Can we come up with a solution together that will make this right?" You can even say, "I want to make this right. How can we do that?"

However, if you have done nothing wrong, don't say sorry. Simply stand by your company's policies and say, "Unfortunately, this is the policy, and you can see it on our website. How can we meet your expectations?"

The customer may have a lot of unreasonable suggestions that you simply can't do. Smile, listen, and then state why you can't meet the customer's expectations. Offer some other solution that is reasonable. It is up to the customer at this point to take your solution or get angry and give up.

Some customers and clients are totally unreasonable. An example that comes to mind includes a friend of mine, who is a dog groomer. A client dropped off a terrier and requested a

Schnauzer cut. My friend performed this cut. When the client returned, she was livid and screamed, "My dog looks horrible! I wanted this and this." She went on to describe a cut that was not a Schnauzer cut at all.

My groomer friend simply had to smile as the client berated her and repeat, "I'm sorry. This is the cut you requested. I will happily groom him differently." The client was not having it, however, and demanded her money back. She insisted that she would go to another groomer who performed better work. In the end, my friend was forced to give the client a refund, and the client still left her a terrible review on Yelp.

The only way my friend was able to mitigate this problem was by replying to the client's review. She apologized again and politely described her side of what happened. Her explanation seemed to do the trick because she didn't lose any business.

The lesson here is that if you try your best to please a client and you can't please him or her, you just have to take the hit. Try to do some sort of damage control, such as replying politely to a bad review. Other people know that some customers are unreasonable and not every negative review on your business is legitimate.

It is also possible to get people to retract bad reviews. You may reach out to a customer and offer to send him or her a free product if he or she removes the review. You can also ask clients to rethink their reviews by offering your side of the situation.

In some cases, such as on your personal website, you can remove bad reviews yourself. Doing this can make you appear dishonest, however, so be careful. Yelp and Google will remove reviews that violate their policies or that come from people who did not actually use your business.

Setting Reasonable Expectations

Every once in a while, you will get clients who demand the world and the moon, as well. You can't please them because they just want more. Some of these clients are not willing to pay for all that they demand, either. While these customers are rare, they do appear now and then—you have to know how to handle them.

I have found absolute transparency is imperative in any industry. By making your business policies and all the things that your services or products include clearly visible to customers, you avoid miscommunication.

When a demanding client wants more than what you can offer for a certain price, you can point out that your prices and services are clearly listed. If they want added services, they must pay for them.

Furthermore, find out exactly what your client wants before providing services. For example, my groomer friend in the above example may have benefited from asking the client for a picture of the cut she wanted before grooming the dog.

Don't assume customers know what they are asking for. Always clarify before performing any service. Ask for details and pictures, if applicable. That way, you can meet the client's expectations or let the client know you can't do something.

Never promise a client more than what you can deliver.

Always set reasonable expectations. "This is what I can do." Make it clear. Then, any issues that arise are out of your hands.

Wrap-Up

Our human clients can be quite difficult. Remember—they just want what is best for their beloved pets. Approach them clearly and fairly and you will be able to defuse most ugly situations. Customer service skills are key to running any business.

The clearer you are with what your business provides in regards to policies, services, etc., the easier it will be to avoid issues with clients.

In the next chapter, I will show you how to get repeat business and promote excellent word-of-mouth referrals. But I would suggest putting the following action steps on a postcard and keeping it handy for when you may need it.

Action Steps

1. Never yell or raise your voice. Never tell a client he or she is wrong.
2. If you are wrong, apologize and ask how you can fix the situation.
3. If you are not wrong, don't apologize and stand firm by your policies.
4. Listen well to figure out how to best handle the situation. Propose reasonable solutions in a calm voice. Invite clients to propose solutions as well and work together.

5. Ask lots of questions to cool clients off and get a full picture of the problem.
6. Try to keep clients from leaving bad reviews.
7. Set reasonable expectations with your clients by being clear and transparent.

34

BUILDING CUSTOMER LOYALTY

Do you like to do business by making a good first impression? When it comes to working in any industry, you want to make such a good impression that people come back and use your services again.

Furthermore, you want people to spread the news—your business is great. Word-of-mouth positive reviews work much better than any other form of advertising for your business. Even if you spend thousands on fancy advertising, you will still get more business from client referrals and reviews.

But how do you get people to come back time and time again? How do you get those positive reviews? Providing the excellent services and customer service your business promises is the first step.

But there are many additional things you can do to make people feel confident about using your business in the future.

Certain little things mean a lot to people and make clients happy.

Free Gifts

Free gifts attract clients and also make them want to come back. To get people to use your services or products, offer some type of free gift as an incentive. This brings the rule of reciprocity into play: Once you give a free gift, at least a few people will feel obligated to purchase something from you.

Just make sure the free gifts won't break your bank! Find something small that you can offer people at little cost to you. Make it something fun or interesting.

Here are some ideas:

- Free nail clippings with first grooming appointment.
- Free one-week trial for a subscription service or information service.
- Access to a free sample of a course or book to get customers to buy the rest. In this case, you want to use a teaser. Offer about twenty percent of the information included in your course, the basic stuff. Then promise they can learn so much more if they purchase the other eighty percent.
- Free sample of pet shampoo with any purchase. If they like it, they will purchase the full-size bottle!
- Free night of boarding if first-time customers book more than five nights or some other number of nights you feel is fair.

- Free bag of dog cookies with purchase of a full-size bag of food.
- Free ten-minute medium or animal communication session for first-time clients.
- Free pamphlet about pet grief, urging customers to sign up for a course or purchase a book to learn more.
- Free fifteen-minute training session for new customers to see if they like your methods.

Discount Programs

My favorite coffeehouse has a program where I get a punch on a card every time I buy a cup of coffee at any of their locations. When I collect ten punches, I get a free cup. Now, this isn't a huge discount, and it probably costs their business a few cents. Yet, it makes me feel as if my patronage is rewarded.

By offering an affordable discount program at your business, you make your clients feel rewarded as well. This encourages repeat business. People will keep coming back to collect the points necessary for that free reward or that percentage discount you promise.

Here are a few examples of how you can apply discounts to your business:

- A rewards program that gives customers points for every item purchased. After a hundred (or some other arbitrary number you set) points, the customer gets one free bag of food or some other product.

- A referral system where a customer gets a free item for every person referred with a special code.
- A punch card for veterinarian visits. After so many visits, a client can get ten percent off his next visit.
- A free acupuncture or massage treatment after referring someone else or spending X-amount of dollars at your business.
- Ten percent off of a second T-shirt or portrait.
- Buy-one-get-one-free deal for your products.
- Twenty percent off customer's first stay in a boarding kennel or first pet walking/drop-in visit.
- Discount codes and coupons for using affiliate links on your blog.
- Free product or visit as a reward for using your company for a year, six months, or some other dedicated amount of time.

Customer Shout-Outs and Engagement

Social media is a great place to engage with clients and customers. It is ideal to be present with your clients so that you form professional relationships with them. Let them know that you care and that you are a real person. It also makes clients and customers feel as if you actually care, so they remember your business with a smile and pass on recommendations.

When people comment on your blog or social media posts, be sure to reply to them. When people ask questions, be sure to answer in a friendly manner. Even when people have negative things to say, be sure to acknowledge their comments and ask

- A referral system where a customer gets a free item for every person referred with a special code.
- A punch card for veterinarian visits. After so many visits, a client can get ten percent off his next visit.
- A free acupuncture or massage treatment after referring someone else or spending X-amount of dollars at your business.
- Ten percent off of a second T-shirt or portrait.
- Buy-one-get-one-free deal for your products.
- Twenty percent off customer's first stay in a boarding kennel or first pet walking/drop-in visit.
- Discount codes and coupons for using affiliate links on your blog.
- Free product or visit as a reward for using your company for a year, six months, or some other dedicated amount of time.

Customer Shout-Outs and Engagement

Social media is a great place to engage with clients and customers. It is ideal to be present with your clients so that you form professional relationships with them. Let them know that you care and that you are a real person. It also makes clients and customers feel as if you actually care, so they remember your business with a smile and pass on recommendations.

When people comment on your blog or social media posts, be sure to reply to them. When people ask questions, be sure to answer in a friendly manner. Even when people have negative things to say, be sure to acknowledge their comments and ask

- Free bag of dog cookies with purchase of a full-size bag of food.
- Free ten-minute medium or animal communication session for first-time clients.
- Free pamphlet about pet grief, urging customers to sign up for a course or purchase a book to learn more.
- Free fifteen-minute training session for new customers to see if they like your methods.

Discount Programs

My favorite coffeehouse has a program where I get a punch on a card every time I buy a cup of coffee at any of their locations. When I collect ten punches, I get a free cup. Now, this isn't a huge discount, and it probably costs their business a few cents. Yet, it makes me feel as if my patronage is rewarded.

By offering an affordable discount program at your business, you make your clients feel rewarded as well. This encourages repeat business. People will keep coming back to collect the points necessary for that free reward or that percentage discount you promise.

Here are a few examples of how you can apply discounts to your business:

- A rewards program that gives customers points for every item purchased. After a hundred (or some other arbitrary number you set) points, the customer gets one free bag of food or some other product.

how you can help. Spend some time each day online looking at and responding to customer feedback.

Shout-outs make loyal customers feel honored. Say someone just buys a ton of one of your products for use in her animal rescue. You can then run a banner on your website or feature her rescue for a month on the front page of your website and mention her in social media posts.

You can also use a system that identifies people who have been loyal to your blog or business for a long period of time, and either post a shout-out to the person on social media, or at the very least, send the person a thank you email.

If you are running a blog, consider engaging with people by running information sessions and live chats. This is where you can answer questions people have. Post that you will be holding a Facebook live on all social media sites and your business site and then attend the live event and chat with your clients, letting them see your face. Bonus points if you show them your own pets!

You can also personally reply to emails and answer questions and concerns people have. By being present and helpful, you make your customers feel as if they are engaging with a real person, not some anonymous Internet robot. This makes them remember you fondly and recommend you to others.

It is not always possible to address every email, so set automatic replies on your email server to acknowledge everyone who emails you. A simple acknowledgement and a promise to reply later is better than silence. As long as you make an effort to reply later when you have the time, your client will appreciate your customer service.

Handwritten Thank You Notes

When someone orders something from you or comes by your business and uses one of your services, always try to send a handwritten thank you note. In your note, always include the client's name and the pet's name.

There are two reasons for doing this:

1. Saying thank you makes customers and clients feel validated.

- Do you enjoy it when a business owner you spend money with thanks you? Absolutely! I know I sure do. Let clients know how much their business means to you and they will want to come back.

1. A handwritten note with the client's and pet's names shows you took time and effort to thank them.

- It means so much more than some automated email or some mass-produced note. To save time, you can mass-produce notes and then sign them personally with the names of your client and his or her pet and then sign with your name. Just adding a touch of personal writing will make the note so much more meaningful.

One of my favorite drop shipping companies will always enclose a handwritten note with a bag of dog cookies taped to it. They pick out the cutest stationery. This free product and handwritten note are probably why I have used them for years.

Go Above and Beyond

If you are running a boarding kennel, your job is pretty straightforward—as long as no issues arise. You board the pet, feed, and exercise. You look after his or her safety. Doing your job without issue will get you at least four stars in a review.

But what gets you five stars is when you go above and beyond.

For example:

1. Give them an extra walk or two.
2. Send unexpected cute pictures of his or her experience at your boarding kennel.
3. Give a massage as a treat.
4. Send them home with a bag of homemade and healthy dog treats.

Find some way to exceed a customer's expectations. Do something a little extra for them. You will make them smile, and they may leave you a better review as a result.

Wrap-Up

There are many wonderful and fun things you can provide your customers. Always keep in mind you want clients and customers to come back. You never want to give them a reason not to return.

The best way to increase your odds of getting repeat business is with the tips and tricks in this chapter. I have used most of them and am always thinking of new and creative ways to say thank you. Check out the action steps below to get you started.

I love giving back to my clients and customers. They appreciate the extra care and thoughtfulness. In turn, I get loyalty, great reviews, and lots of recommendations.

Action Steps

1. Implement some of the free gifts suggested in this chapter—if they are appropriate for your business.
2. Come up with some of your own unique ideas that your customers or clients would love.
3. Consider offering a discount or rewards program—if appropriate with your business brand.
4. Post about great clients on social media or in a newsletter.
5. Always do special things for your clients and customers. Go above and beyond—it always pays off with reviews and loyalty.
6. Send handwritten thank you notes with purchases. People love handwritten notes even in the digital age.

PEP TALK!

Are you beyond excited to begin your chosen pet career? Have you done the action steps to organize your goals, educational plan, and business ideas? Are you ready to finally do something you love every single day?

If you love pets, you will love working with them and for them. The pet industry is a multibillion-dollar industry that shows even more expansion in upcoming years. You deserve to be happy with what you do, but you must also make enough to survive! Fortunately, the pet industry has a special place for you.

Working with animals is fun and rewarding, but it does come with some challenges. Your new career is just beginning, but always remember the possibilities are endless. If you feel like you are going to give up…don't. Instead, be creative. Think of a new service you could offer. Get more education. Get involved locally for animals in need.

There are endless opportunities when choosing a pet career. Depending on your choice, you can create a viable way to make a living for yourself. The other benefit is you will be part of the pet industry—helping to make the world a better place for animals and their people.

Your work is a vehicle for new ideas, promoting your views, generating business, and building a brand that your clients will love and trust. Never forget this.

- Start making your dream career come true with this book.

- This is the starting point.
- The next step is up to you.

If you have the desire to work with animals, then you should absolutely make it happen! You won't regret it. I know I never regretted chasing my dreams to work with animals—*never!*

> *I am so proud of you for taking the steps to fill your life with animals. I wish you great success and happiness on your journey. You will be successful as long as you put your mind to it and don't let anything stop you!*

Warmly,

Wendy Van de Poll

October, 2019

All books in The Pet Biz Series

- Pet Blogging 101: How to Start a Riveting Pet Blog and Gain Loyal Followers, (Book 1)
- Pet Jobs 101: How to Choose your Dream Job and Jumpstart Your Business. (Book 2)
- Pet Authorpreneur 101: How to Become a Successful Pet Author and Grow Your Business, (Book 3)

- This is the starting point.
- The next step is up to you.

If you have the desire to work with animals, then you should absolutely make it happen! You won't regret it. I know I never regretted chasing my dreams to work with animals—*never*!

> *I am so proud of you for taking the steps to fill your life with animals. I wish you great success and happiness on your journey. You will be successful as long as you put your mind to it and don't let anything stop you!*

Warmly,

Wendy Van de Poll

October, 2019

All books in The Pet Biz Series

- Pet Blogging 101: How to Start a Riveting Pet Blog and Gain Loyal Followers, (Book 1)
- Pet Jobs 101: How to Choose your Dream Job and Jumpstart Your Business. (Book 2)
- Pet Authorpreneur 101: How to Become a Successful Pet Author and Grow Your Business, (Book 3)

PEP TALK!

Are you beyond excited to begin your chosen pet career? Have you done the action steps to organize your goals, educational plan, and business ideas? Are you ready to finally do something you love every single day?

If you love pets, you will love working with them and for them. The pet industry is a multibillion-dollar industry that shows even more expansion in upcoming years. You deserve to be happy with what you do, but you must also make enough to survive! Fortunately, the pet industry has a special place for you.

Working with animals is fun and rewarding, but it does come with some challenges. Your new career is just beginning, but always remember the possibilities are endless. If you feel like you are going to give up…don't. Instead, be creative. Think of a new service you could offer. Get more education. Get involved locally for animals in need.

There are endless opportunities when choosing a pet career. Depending on your choice, you can create a viable way to make a living for yourself. The other benefit is you will be part of the pet industry—helping to make the world a better place for animals and their people.

Your work is a vehicle for new ideas, promoting your views, generating business, and building a brand that your clients will love and trust. Never forget this.

- Start making your dream career come true with this book.

GLOSSARY

Affiliate Links – Or affiliate marketing is a type of marketing in which one business rewards another business (affiliate) for each visitor and/or purchase by that visitor. It is up to the affiliate to market. A special link is provided by the company the affiliate is promoting.

Amazon Algorithms – A complicated system by Amazon. Their layers of algorithms determine how books are ranked in the best-seller charts, popularity list, which books appear in the keyword search and the order in which they appear.

Animal Mediumship – Is another term for "animal communicator"; a person who has the ability to speak to animals that have died. Some animal communicators may speak to animals in spirit but not all. Many animal communicators offer both or specialize.

Blended Degree – A hybrid course designed to provide students with instruction through classroom sessions as well as online. Blended courses/degrees give you control over the place, time and pace of classes.

Blog - Blog posts are the fundamental of a blog. Every blog on the internet consists of different blog posts written by the blogger. ... Blogs (and blog posts) can be shared on social networks (Twitter, Facebook, etc.) and people can leave comments under the blog posts in order to start meaningful conversations.

Branding – The marketing practice of creating a name and logo that identifies your product from others. A great brand strategy gives your business a major edge in competitive market. It is your promise to your customers' needs.

Contact Widget — A contact widget is basically an add-on in your WordPress site. It allows your visitors to communicate with you via email when it is filled out.

Crystal Healing — When holding crystals or placing them on various parts of the body they promote physical, emotional, and spiritual healing. They do this by positively interacting with your body's energy field.

Energy Medicine — Is defined as any energetic or informational interaction with a biological system to bring back balance in the body. For example: Crystal Healing, Reiki, and Flower Essences.

Flower Essences — Liquid extracts used to address issues of emotional, physical, and spiritual well-being. They are part of energy medicine which includes: homeopathy, acupuncture, color therapy, crystal healing, Reiki, etc.

Google Keyword Planner — A tool that provides keyword ideas and traffic estimates to help you build traffic to your website.

Hashtags - A hashtag is a label for content. It helps others who are interested in a certain topic find content on that same topic. A hashtag looks something like this: #wendyvandepoll or #dogsoninstagram. Hashtags are used mostly on social media sites. They rocketed to fame on Twitter.

Homeopathy — The practice of holistic energy medicine. It is a natural approach to treatment of physical ailments, as well as, emotional and spiritual. Created in 1796 by Samuel

Hahnemann. It is based on his doctrine of like cures all disease or a substance that causes the symptoms of a disease in a healthy person would cure similar symptoms in sick people.

Hosting Ads – The practice of promoting an affiliate product on your website. You join another company's affiliate program. You place a banner on your website to sell these products. You can either post for free or charge the company. It depends on the affiliate contract.

Keyword/ Short-tailed Keyword – Short tail keywords are search phrases with only one or two words. Their length makes them less specific than searches with more words. "Pet" (one word) is an example of a short tail keyword, whereas "holistic raw cat food" (four words) is a long tail keyword.

Long-tailed Keyword/ Keyword Phrase - A keyword phrase is two or more words typed as a search query. For example, "What is the best way to feed my senior cat" is a good example of a keyword phrase.

Optimize – On your website you add relevant keywords and phrases, meta tags, image tags, and other components to ensure it is accessible to a search engine and improves the over chances your website will be indexed by search engines.

Reiki – An energy medicine healing technique based on the principle that the therapist can channel energy into the client by means of touch. This will activate the natural healing process of the client's body, mind, and spirit.

SEO - SEO or Search Engine Optimization is the name given to activity that attempts to improve search engine rankings. In search results Google™ displays links to pages it considers optimal according to your keywords.

Search Engine – A program that searches for and identifies items in a data base that correspond to keywords or characters specified by the user, used especially for finding particular sites on the World Wide Web.

Universal Energy – Is the basis of our entire existence. It is the energy that sustains life and provides vital energy to all living systems.

Website - a group of World Wide Web pages usually containing hyperlinks to each other and made available online by an individual, company, educational institution, government, or organization.

RESOURCES

A FREE GIFT

A Complete List of over 150 Animal Resource Sites including but not limited to:
Animal Training
Grooming
Veterinary and Veterinary Technician
Wildlife Rehabilitator
Animal Reiki
Animal Massage
And MORE!

Here is your link to download:
https://wendyvandepoll.com/pet-jobs-free-gift

****You can also get the following links
in your free gift that you downloaded above.****

Books in The Pet Biz Series

Pet Blogging 101: How to Start a Riveting Pet Blog and Gain Loyal Followers
https://amazon.com/dp/B07XWRS95W

Pet Jobs 101: How to Choose your Dream Job and Jumpstart Your Business

Pet Authorpreneur 101: How to Become a Successful Pet Author and Grow Your Business

AFFILIATE SITES

ConvertKit - email provider
https://wendyvandepoll.com/convert-kit

ProWritingAid - editing software
https://wendyvandepoll.com/pro-writing-aid

Self-Publishing School – self-publish your book platform
https://wendyvandepoll.com/self-publishing-school

Siteground - website host
https://wendyvandepoll.com/siteground

Teachable – course host
https://wendyvandepoll.com/teachable

DROP SHIPPING MARKET PLACE

Aliexpress
https://azliexpress.com

Spocket
https://spocket.co

Pet Jobs 101: How to Choose your Dream Job and Jumpstart Your Business

Pet Authorpreneur 101: How to Become a Successful Pet Author and Grow Your Business

AFFILIATE SITES

ConvertKit - email provider
https://wendyvandepoll.com/convert-kit

ProWritingAid - editing software
https://wendyvandepoll.com/pro-writing-aid

Self-Publishing School – self-publish your book platform
https://wendyvandepoll.com/self-publishing-school

Siteground - website host
https://wendyvandepoll.com/siteground

Teachable – course host
https://wendyvandepoll.com/teachable

DROP SHIPPING MARKET PLACE

Aliexpress
https://azliexpress.com

Spocket
https://spocket.co

RESOURCES

A FREE GIFT

A Complete List of over 150 Animal Resource Sites including but not limited to:
Animal Training
Grooming
Veterinary and Veterinary Technician
Wildlife Rehabilitator
Animal Reiki
Animal Massage
And MORE!

Here is your link to download:
https://wendyvandepoll.com/pet-jobs-free-gift

****You can also get the following links
in your free gift that you downloaded above.****

Books in The Pet Biz Series

Pet Blogging 101: How to Start a Riveting Pet Blog and Gain Loyal Followers
https://amazon.com/dp/B07XWRS95W

Printful
https://printful.com

Doba
https://www.inventorysource.com

Oberlo
https://oberlo.com

GRAPHIC DESIGN SITES

Canva
https://canva.com

PicMonkey
https://picmonkey.com

MULTI-LEVEL MARKETING

Life Abundance
https://lifesabundance.com

pawTree
https://www.pawtree.com

Nevetica
https://nevetica.com

HB Naturals
https://hbnaturals.com

PHOTOS

Pixabay
https://pixabay.com

Librestock
https://librestock.com

Deposit Photos
https://depositphotos.com

SERVICES

Guru
https://guru.com

Upwork
https://upwork.com

Fiverr
http://fiverr.com

SCORE
https://score.org

Smashwords
https://smashwords.com

Vistaprint
https://vistaprint.com

SHOPS TO HOST YOUR PRODUCTS

Amazon
https://services.amazon.com

Rush Order Tees
https://rushordertees.com

Shutterfly
https://shutterfly.com

Stitchfix
https://stitchfix.com

SOCIAL MEDIA ORGANIZATIONAL TOOLS

Agora Pulse
https://agorapulse.com

Buffer
https://buffer.com

Hootsuite
https://hootsuite.com

Later
https://later.com

ShareCount
https://www.sharedcount.com

SUPPLIES

Frontier Coop Wholesale
https://wholesale.frontiercoop.com

OTHER

Spirit Paw Academy
https://spiritpawacademy.teachable.com

If you would like even more links!
Please download my free list of over 150 links to pet careers, pet-related job, organizations, and much more.
https://wendyvandepoll.com/pet-jobs-free-gift

The **recommended sites are products that I use and highly recommend. They are affiliate links which means if you purchase the product, I receive a small commission (which helps me greatly as an author.) You are not charged more because of the affiliate link.

ACKNOWLEDGEMENTS

I would like to thank all the animals who have trusted me to be their advocate and voice. They inspire me to be the best human-being I possibly can.

Many thanks go to my followers, students, and clients. Thank you for pushing me to write this book and others to follow in this series. It takes a team to put together a book and I would like to extend my appreciation to all that have helped along the way.

A huge hug goes to my husband, Rick. He is a remarkable animal lover and human being who dedicates his life to the animals and the environment. He inspires my soul. You can find his books on Amazon, as well.

ABOUT THE AUTHOR

Animals are Wendy Van de Poll's passion. Any chance she gets she is hiking with her dog, observing wildlife in her backwoods, and listening to their wisdom.

Wendy Van de Poll is an award-winning and International best-selling author of thirteen books and counting. She has been working with animals in various capacities for over forty years. With her success she is passionate about helping others achieve their writing and pet business goals.

Wendy has helped people around the world start their own blogging sites, pet businesses, and write best-selling books. Her clients describe Wendy as a "dedicated partner who helps get your ideas down on paper, your work (blog, job, or book) done, and in the hands of readers and customers who want more."

She is the founder of the CenterforPetLossGrief.com. Her website and blog provide a safe place for dedicated pet parents and pet professionals who want support and guidance with pet loss grief, hospice for pets, and coping with the loss of their pets.

Wendy is a certified end-of-life and grief coach and a tested animal communicator and medium.

She holds a Master of Science degree in wolf ecology and behavior and has run with wild wolves in Minnesota, coyotes in Massachusetts, and foxes in her backyard.

Wendy also coaches people who want write their own books about their pets and other topics.

Her articles can be seen on Medium.com as well as her own websites.

Her articles can be seen on:

Wendy Van de Poll, Bestselling Author, Influencer, Animal Advocate: https://wendyvandepoll.com

Center For Pet Loss Grief, LLC: https://centerforpetloss-grief.com

Medium.com: https://medium.com/@wendyvandepoll

Click Here to Get Your Free Gift:

https://wendyvandepoll.com/pet-jobs-free-gift

Pet Jobs 101
How to Choose Your Dream Job and Jumpstart Your Business

THANK YOU!

As the author of this book, I appreciate you buying and reading it. I hope you found the information useful and are on your way to choosing your dream job and starting your business.

I would be grateful if you would leave a helpful book review, either with your favorite book distributor or with Amazon.

Thank you,

Wendy Van de Poll, MS, CEOL

Best-selling and Award-winning Author, Writing Coach, Animal Advocate

www.wendyvandepoll.com

For all of Wendy Van de Poll's books, please visit:
https:amazon.com/author/wendyvandepoll

Check out my Free Gift that Goes with This Book
https://wendyvandepoll.com/pet-jobs-free-gift

ALSO BY WENDY VAN DE POLL

The Pet Biz Series

Pet Blogging 101

Pet Jobs 101

Pet Authorpreneur 101

Pet Bereavement Series

My Dog Is Dying: What Do I Do?

My Dog Has Died: What Do I Do?

My Cat Is Dying: What Do I Do?

My Cat Has Died: What Do I Do?

Healing a Child's Pet Loss Grief

The Pet Professional's Guide to Pet Loss

Pet Loss Poems: To Heal Your Heart and Soul

Human-Animal Books

Animal Wisdom: Conversations From The Heart Between Animals and Their People

Free Book

Healing Your Heart From Pet Loss Grief

Children's Picture Books

The Adventures of Ms. Addie Pants Series

The Rescue

The Ice Storm

New Friends

Off to School

To receive notification when more books are published, please go to:

https://wendyvandepoll.com.

We will add you to the mailing list after you download your free gift.

You can also find my books on Amazon:

https://amazon.com/author/wendyvandepoll